THE RESPONSE LEADERSHIP SEQUENCE™

Empowering and Improving Your Leadership Before, During, and After a Crisis

Mike McKenna

Cover designed by Cover Designer

Mike McKenna/TEAM Solutions
Visit my website at www.TEAM-Solutions.US

Printed in the United States of America

First Printing: Dec 2017
TEAM Solutions

ISBN- 978-1-973-51903-4

I dedicate this book to all Response Leaders who head toward a crisis while everyone else runs away from it.

"We can only do what we're trained to do. And everything we do is training us for something."

—MIKE MCKENNA

Contents

What is Response Leadership?

"*Shi Paku*" is a Japanese phrase that loosely means "*4 whites.*" It describes a condition where the white sclera in our eyes involuntarily appears above and below our iris that's contracted as a reaction to extreme stress.

When someone is experiencing this level of stress, the sight is unmistakable.

We've experienced or can imagine a similar stress reaction:

- Waking up from a nightmare about being naked in front of our peers or trying to whistle the song "Dixie" in 28-degree weather.
- Treating someone special to a first date and realizing when the bill arrives that our wallet is at home.
- Going toward a high-risk environment with unknown hazards, while others are going the opposite direction in an effort to escape.
- Being promoted to an unfamiliar position, to immediately lead an unsupportive team, through a difficult function, in view of the critical boss.

Response Leaders on the other hand seldom experience *Shi Paku*. They learn to react to the stresses of life's planned and unplanned events with *competence*, *comprehension*, and *confidence*.

Response Leaders understand that to survive and thrive during these events; they must be a strong leader for themselves before they can be a strong leader around others.

Therefore:

Response Leadership is the ability to lead oneself and others during their response to any event of any size or complexity.

If you go toward a crisis instead of away from it, this leadership program is your secret weapon.

* * *

Origin of Response Leadership

Response Leadership represents over 20 years of experience in leading and responding to planned and unplanned events. Learn more about me here: https://team-solutions.us/who-we-are/

I'm fortunate to have gained a broad base of experience in several different industries in both in the private and public sectors.

Within the tremendous diversity of these experiences, a common theme also developed: the struggle to develop strong leaders, particularly when times were tough.

The hunger for competent, balanced and capable leaders is everywhere and crosses every segment of a professional organization.

A few years ago, I started collecting data on leadership. Not just quotes, platitudes, and bumper stickers, but actual, make-a-difference-when-it-mattered type leadership data.

What I discovered was that no single industry had it figured out. Everyone seemed to be grappling with how to build and transform competent leaders.

So, I decided to merge what I had learned and understood so far about leadership in the different segments within both the public and private sectors.

After uniting the applicable leadership concepts I'd collected, I then sought to simplify them so that they were readily acceptable to the very people and organizations that needed them, wherever they may be.

- If you have the responsibility to go TOWARD a crisis when everyone else goes AWAY from them, this material is for you.
- If you want to be more confident and knowledgeable about your job, this material is for you.

This program directly tackles the common problems I noted that persist across most organizations. In this program, I provide solutions for the current and insufficient approach to managing an incident, including criticisms such as:

- *Poor communication*
- *Lack of accountability and ambiguous supervision*
- *Absence of an effective, proven planning and management process*
- *Poor teamwork and low levels of engagement*
- *Disparate "silos" of different groups, facilities, equipment, and communications*
- *Top-heavy command and control, not enough coordination with the people doing the work*
- *Planned events that turn into unplanned emergencies*
- *Systems (like ICS) that are too complicated, too many acronyms*
- *Concepts and differences that are misfits for typical business activity*
- *Not enough volunteer support*
- *Difficult to achieve a common operating picture*
- *Consultants and trainers who want to make managing an incident look hard*
- *Lack of performers who are experienced, not just trained*
- *Lack of leadership during complex incidents*
- *Lack of inclusion of all stakeholders, including non-governmental organizations (NGOs)*
- *More response coordination and less power management*
- *Too much awareness training, not enough proficiency training*
- *Too much method, not enough management*
- *Lack of Leadership, trust, ownership, and communications*

Response Leadership addresses All-Hazards, which is a fancy way of saying that it doesn't just provide what you need to successfully respond to and lead a **cyber intrusion** *or* **a bake sale** but it will help you successfully respond to and lead a cyber intrusion **AND** a bake sale.

To bring you this definitive guide, I've drawn the most applicable parts of the following sources and first-hand experiences:

- National Incident Management System (NIMS) Compliance: Incident Command System (ICS) 100, 200, 300, 400, 700, 800, ICS for School, ICS for Hospitals and others
- All-Hazard Incident Management Team (AHIMT) Training and Preparedness (including National Planning Scenarios)
- Enhanced Incident Management & Unified Command
- Business Continuity Management (BCM), including Cyber Response

- Project Management Best Practices
- Extensive surveying of clients and other experienced Response Leaders
- Leadership development best practices
- Crisis and Event management best practices
- Plus ... 20+ years of Response Leadership experience!

As mentioned above, part of this Response Leadership sequence is adapted from the battle-tested Incident Command System (ICS) used by emergency responders since the early 1970's and from the US Military since WWII.

- ICS is currently the US national standard for managing an incident under the National Incident Management System (NIMS), which is the doctrine mandated since 2005 to help create a secure and resilient nation.
- "ICS translations" will be provided throughout this program when there are notable ICS-inspired references used. The purpose of this is two-fold:

    o Provide material that is reasonably consistent with a national standard.
    o Provide a basis for when ICS practitioners need to interact with your event.

This program represents my best work to-date on how to transform yourself and others into world-class Response Leaders.

Frequently Asked Questions (F.A.Q.) and Key Assumptions:

Is everything an event and everyone a Response Leader?

Almost. If you're lying on the couch watching a Law & Order marathon, Response Leadership skills may not be needed, but to build proficiency, we will apply a Response Leadership filter to nearly everything else.

Isn't leadership training a 'soft skill'?

Most of it, yes. Not this program, though. Becoming a better Response Leader is not a soft skill, it's a duffel bag full of hard skills that help you transform yourself, your peers and your organization.

Is this new material or rehashed material?

Both. Much of the knowledge, the science, the application and the lessons on how to improve leadership has been around in various forms for a while, just poorly packaged. The problem confronting most of us is how to identify and take advantage of the best parts of that research to quickly comprehend and apply it to our real lives. If that were already being done, I wouldn't have been compelled to create this program. This program is assembled and presented to today's demanding learner.

Why should I take leadership advice from someone that doesn't have to deal with the consequences?

Fair question. The decision to improve your leadership is a personal one. Even being limited in how far I can travel on that journey with you, make no mistake, I'm putting my personal and professional reputation at risk by guaranteeing that this program will improve your leadership.

Doesn't hiring a leadership consultant, trainer or facilitator mean that I don't understand my organization?

Sometimes, sure. Ponder this though: The last time my air conditioner stopped cooling my house, I called an HVAC professional to fix the right things, faster and more reliably than I could have by myself watching hours of YouTube videos. One of the first acts of the success-minded is knowing when to bring in outside people to help.

What's the meaning of an "event"?

Planned events (parade, tournament, etc.) and unplanned events, or incidents (tornado, computer breach, etc.) are "events" since managing them is almost identical.

Even if I'm in charge, won't other people just handle it?

Response leaders are responsible for everything until everything gets delegated. Then they're responsible for everything **and** the delegate.

Is this program compliant with (___fill in the blank___) standard?

In the consequential world of response, **competence** is more valuable than **compliance**. The outcome of this program is the creation of increased proficiency. Since it represents a collection of material from many disciplines, currently there is no applicable certification standard. Users will be able to immediately excel and 'test-out' of many of those other courses though.

What if we have a guy named Martin that does all of this for us already?

Martin is a name, not a function. The function takes precedence over the name of the person performing the function. When the person leaves, the function remains. And when the function remains, the job gets done.

Is this program the only way to improve Response Leadership?

It's the only place currently to learn Response Leadership. However, it is "a tool, not the tool." This program also provides guidance, not policy.

Is this program based on the author's inference, experience, and instinct or is it based on quantitative and qualitative data?

Both. Findings are gathered and presented from case studies that highlight 'lessons learned,' from interviewing hundreds of Response Leaders and from my own, ongoing successes and struggles as a leader.

Does it require a huge, spread-out organization?

No. Response Leadership is a scalable system; it expands only to use what is needed. Response Leaders manage events at the lowest possible level of a hierarchy.

Will I receive specific tactics to use for my event?

In a general sense, yes. Specifically, unlikely. The focus is on learning the process, not specific tactics. Examples are broken down for illustration purposes, not to complicate every decision.

Best practices? Really?

Best practices are called that for a reason. Buzzword aside, I'm presenting the very best way to competently lead through a planned or unplanned event, based on over 20 years of experience. If or when I find a better way, I'll change this material to reflect that!

Isn't this kind of training just for First Responders, like police and fire?

Everyone is a first responder. Long before emergency services arrive, there is plenty that you can and should do, and this program equips you to do that.

Is this the perfect program for me to become a better leader?

The perfect event doesn't exist. Neither does the perfect program. My commitment is to deliver the most relevant and accurate information possible to help you become a better Response Leader. As I've done during my whole career, when I learn a better way, I will update the information to reflect that. That's regardless if I learned it from you, from my first-hand experiences or from reading it off a bathroom wall. Okay, maybe not the last one.

Is this program NIMS compliant?

Yes. NIMS refers to the National Incident Management System, which is a U.S. government construct intended to provide a "consistent framework for incident management" for the public, private and government sectors to "work together to prevent, protect against, respond to, recover from, and mitigate the effects of incidents regardless of cause, size, location, or complexity." The NIMS still-unfinished doctrine represents a "core set of concepts, principles, terminology, and organizational processes that enable effective, efficient, and collaborative incident management." This program does its part by sharing best practices across all sectors, including the Incident Command System (ICS). You can read more about NIMS and the presidential directive that requires its use at FEMA.gov and search "NIMS."

What will I be able to do after completing this program?

You will have the knowledge, awareness, and many of the skills needed to serve in a position of leadership in any size event, whether planned or unplanned.

Specifically, becoming a practitioner of Response Leadership will assist you in the areas of:

1. Planning, Equipping, Training, Evaluating before the event
2. Maximizing the use of a collaborative and functional-based management system
3. Centralized coordination of different people, places, and things
4. Organizing tasks and strategies in a standardized, modular structure
5. Delegating responsibility AND defined lines of authority
6. Improved, relevant communications
7. Assessing and evaluating progress and making consistent improvements
8. And much, much more.

Any questions, at any time, will get answered by connecting with me through my website: https://team-solutions.us

Response Leader Mindset

"Everything can be taken from a man but one thing: the last of the human freedoms -- to choose one's attitude in any given set of circumstances, to choose one's own way." ~ Viktor Frankl

---

Remember, Response Leadership is a mindset, not a label.

When I was in high-school, I was a wrestler. Our coach was tough, our practices were physical, and our bodies were banged up. The trainer at the time treated every injury, big or small, with a bag of ice. Not just at the onset of an injury, but that was his entire course of treatment. It took a late-night trip to the emergency room to discover the extent of my torn muscles and dislocated knee-cap, costing me valuable time for a swift recovery.

The Iceman's mindset was limited and inflexible.

To avoid these limitations and to maximize the chance of success, Response Leaders must also expand their mindset.

"95% of this game is half mental." ~ Yogi Berra

Having a Response Leader mindset is based on the belief that having and using different mental models can improve our outcomes.

So, what are mental models, exactly?

Mental Models

"The mind is everything. What you think you become." ~ *Buddha*

Mental models fundamentally define our view of the world, provide immediate results, and enable better decision-making.

Most likely our very first mental models were introduced to us by our parents:

"Don't talk to strangers."
"Don't take wooden nickels."
"Don't eat the yellow snow."

Rules for life, they told us.

Thankfully, as we matured, our understanding of these 'rules' expanded and deepened on how best to apply them.

For instance, not eating something yellow that's supposed to be white remains a widely applicable and germane guide to decision-making. However, I'm told that pointing and yelling "stranger danger!" is not an acceptable way to meet your new boss on your first day of work.

When cognitive scientists started researching and categorizing these 'rules for living,' they discovered that these 'rules' were most valuable when viewed more as a framework or model than as doctrine.

Think of mental models as the trunk of a tree and all of our various activities and experiences are the branches, twigs, and leaves. By having a solid trunk of fundamental knowledge, all subsequent growth can develop.

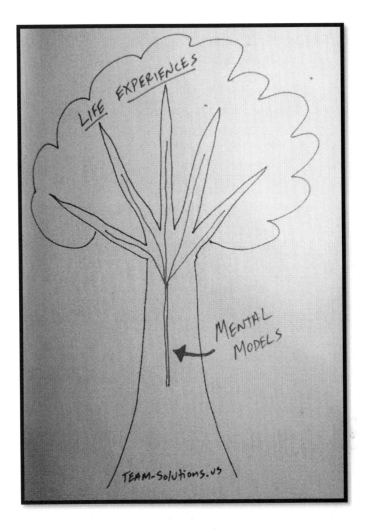

Since mental models fuel our fundamental views of the world, I'm confident that you already rely on some of them.

- Do you buy higher quality items because you believe they will last longer? That's a model called the *"Cost-Benefit Analysis."*
- Do you relate to the TV show that features couples selecting a new home from three available choices? They use a model called the *"Paradox of Choice,"* which reduces anxiety in decision making by reducing the number of available choices.

- As a matter of policy do you tell your kids to stand a few feet back from the street at intersections? That's a model called the *"Margin of Safety"* and is likely your default approach to managing other risks.

As our knowledge, experience and confidence increase, our ability to adapt and apply these mental models to multiple disciplines can also increase.

Here are some examples how having a foundation in the above models is leveraged into other areas and disciplines:

- Using your "Cost-Benefit Analysis" mental model, you can also:
  - implement sensible work policy,
  - make optimal education choices, and
  - safely evacuate flood victims.

- Using your "Paradox of Choice" mental model, you can also:
  - pick out toothpaste,
  - decide on where to spend your summer vacation, and
  - determine where to assign resources to help people in need.

- Using your "Margin of Safety" mental model, you can also:
  - reduce the risk inherent to driving,
  - investing, and
  - crisis response.

Knowing the name of the mental model is not nearly as important as acknowledging their usefulness in other areas of our life.

And therein lies the magic of mental models. The more familiar we are in how they shape our view of the world, the more potent our confidence and competence as Response Leaders become.

To that end, here are some of my current rules for living (a/k/a mental models) that helped form the basis of this book:

"Do the most good for the most people as quickly and safely as possible."
[Effective Altruism and Pareto Efficiency]

"How you do one thing is how you do everything."
[Core Competency]

"If it's predictable, it's preventable."
[Probability and Bayes' Theorem]

"Passion, Purpose and The Wheel of Engagement™."
[Cialdini's Six Principles of Influence]

"Move people from a bad place to a better place, not a bad place to a worse place."
[The Cobra Effect and the Law of Unintended Consequences]

"To maximize performance, Leaders communicate clear objectives, provide tangible support and remove any obstacles."
[Pygmalion Effect]

"Make decisions based on your strengths and delegate the rest."
[Circle of Competence]

"Engagement levels operate like a pendulum."
[Regression to the Mean]

"99% of all funny YouTube videos are attributed to the laws of gravity or inertia."
[Newton's Laws of Motion and Universal Gravitation]

"Those who understand more principles/mental models well know how to interact with the world more effectively than those who know fewer of them or know them less well." ~ Ray Dalio

---

Furthermore, having a tool bag full of diverse mental models can help Response Leader's provide diverse solutions to complex problems. By using these cognitive biases, they can conserve the mental energy needed to update their beliefs.

More about the downside of these biases in a moment.

Below are some additional examples of common and useful mental models:

Occam's Razor: Among various theories, picking the one with the least number of assumptions. I.e., *"The barking we hear is more likely a dog, not a seal."*

Cost-Benefit Analysis: Estimating the strengths and weaknesses of alternatives. I.e., *"Should we hire new staff, or assign more work to the existing staff?"*

Selection Bias: Selecting people, things, data, etc. that reduces randomization or diversity. I.e., *"Let's pick other firefighters to staff this command post instead of bringing in other people with too many divergent perspectives."*

Bayes' Theorem: Determining the probability of an event or outcome based on conditions related to that event. I.e., *"Residents of that community are much older, and few have cars. Therefore, they need more assistance to evacuate."*

Opportunity Cost: Making a choice between the better of mutually exclusive alternatives, missing out on the benefits of the second choice. I.e., *"If we solve Problem A first, Problem B may worsen due to not being solved."*

Confirmation Bias: Interpreting information that confirms pre-existing beliefs, while discarding other alternatives. I.e., *"Nobody can survive after being trapped in that little space."*

Dunning–Kruger effect: Mistaking our ability to be greater than it is. Similarly, assuming that tasks easy for us are also easy for others. I.e. *"He attended one training session and now presents himself as being highly competent."*

According to Shane Parrish at the *Farnam Street Blog*, there are over 100 different mental models that leaders throughout time have and continue to use. In addition to those already stated, I also base my content on many more of the common, practical models that Response Leaders use.

Unknown Unknowns	**Cognitive Biases**
Strategy v. Tactics	**Systems Thinking**
Exit Strategy	**Survivorship Bias**

Succeeding with mental-models requires:

- Having lots of them to reference
- They must be foundational, as in, not temporary

As you see, Response Leaders must not only know and have mental models, but they must develop them through deliberate practice and purposeful application. As you read through the Response Leadership Sequence™ be on the lookout for these mental frameworks that you want or need to adopt, adapt or accelerate their use.

"Developing the habit of mastering the multiple models which underlie reality is the best thing you can do. " ~ *Charlie Munger, Berkshire Hathaway*

Next, let's look at some of the challenges Response Leaders face when trying to establish a positive and productive mindset.

Mindset Challenges

"A real leader faces the music, even when he doesn't like the tune." ~ Anonymous

---

When Response Leaders struggle during his/her leadership of an event, there tend to be four common causes.

By first identifying and understanding these causes, we can take steps to reduce the likelihood of them impacting our next event.

#1 - Response Leadership based on FEAR.

- The Response Leader's fear, not the fear within his/her team.
- The Response Leader's fight or flight instinct - based on the Response Leader's fears.
- The Response Leader needs to know that quitting is not an option, failure is human and effort is worthwhile.

#2 - Response Leadership that makes decisions too SLOWLY.

- The Response Leader stifles feedback and communication.
- The Response Leader keeps a tight inner circle of like minds.

#3 - Response Leadership that makes decisions too QUICKLY.

- The Response Leader doesn't use enough critical thinking skills.
- In his intellectual book *Thinking, Fast and Slow*, author Daniel Kahneman refers to quick, error-prone thinking as System 1 thinking and methodical, informed thinking as System 2 thinking.
- By making decisions too quickly, the Response Leader is acting impulsively, and their error rate will be high.

#4 - Response Leadership that communicates POORLY.

- The Response Leader doesn't take steps to control the message
- The Response Leader doesn't engender support from the troops (social cohesion)
- The Response Leader only speaks up in when opposition to something

---

"Chance favours the prepared mind." ~Louis Pasteur

The best solution to these challenges is mental preparation. A sharpening of the Response Leader brain is required.

Situation-based training provides for the sights and sounds of an event to be imprinted in the Response Leader's hippocampus (part of the brain the imprints long-term memories).

Then, when an event occurs, particularly one that is unplanned, our brains will search for a matching experience from one of our existing mental models.

For example:

Part of a strip mall collapses during a significant weather event. Based on our foundation using Occam's Razor; among various theories, pick the one with the least number of assumptions. An example is: *"The barking we hear is more likely a dog, not a seal."* Therefore, we assume that the significant weather event caused the collapse – *just like our experience last year during a storm* - and not an escaped pachyderm from the zoo looking for a sandwich.

When our brain syncs up those experiences from last year's collapse and the current collapse, it will seamlessly deliver the response that already exists in the recesses of our mind.

Unfortunately, if it doesn't find a comparable experience to draw from, panic takes over in the form of aggression (fight response) or inaction (flight response).

The fix is to simply create those long-term memories (the sights, sounds, and experiences of an event) before the event actually happens.

How?

- Formally, by participating in situation-based training. Like this program.

- Informally, by imagining the event and extensively role-playing your part in it.

The book *The Survivors Club: The Secrets and Science that Could Save Your Life* by Ben Sherwood provides compelling evidence of this.

Story after harrowing story illustrates that the mindset of having 'been there before' was a common reason that victims survived a terrible event (bear attack, plane crash, etc.) while most victims did not.

Now let's explore some of the attributes of a Response Leader's mental mindset.

Innovation

"The world leaders in innovation and creativity will also be world leaders in everything else." ~ Harold R. McAlindon

---

Innovation is a popular leadership topic these days. It gathered steam not long after the topic of "change" became a hot topic.

However, seldom discussed much is:

- why is a change needed in the first place and
- what do they hope to accomplish with that change?

Do Why and What sound familiar?

Even more challenging is the chorus of "we're not changing because that's the way we've always done it!"

Innovation promoted by innovators became the fuel to affect that change.

And the co-conspirators in this 'innovate to affect change' strategy is the use of new or emerging technology.

"Our people are not engaged so we must change our strategy by being innovative. Effective immediately, we're issuing them all new tablet computers so that employees can video conference each other more easily on the weekends."

Does that sound like a well-executed decision that solves a known problem?

Innovations have an extraordinary burden to overcome:

The innovation must deliver an improved condition, as in:

"We had this solution ... now we have this better solution."

Innovations should deliver on the following promises:

- optimize current processes
- solve a problem
- reduce complexity and waste

Innovation Examples:

- Elon Musk/TESLA, innovating how we power our cars and homes
- Uber, innovating how we get around
- Airbnb, innovating how we vacation
- Marriott Hotel, innovating how we check in
- Gutenberg, innovating how we access the written word

So how does a Response Leader innovate? The same standards apply:

1. Consider the unintended consequences.
2. Any innovations must make the condition better.

Governmental emergency responses often rely on antiquated orders, contingency plans, and procedures.

While these tried and true methods are still mostly successful, the layers of bureaucracy in most government agencies prove to be a powerful deterrent to innovation.

Example:

A governmental attempt to use technology to innovate how location data gets captured, collected, and shared by disaster responders has made it harder and more burdensome to capture, collect, and share the data.

Example:

Some car rental companies have embraced a technology that uses a radio frequency emitted from a handheld fob to start the car. For it to work, the fob must be within a few feet of the car, such as in the driver's pocket.

An actual key is not being used to open the door nor is it put into an ignition. Because those actions don't lead to habituation, the rate of loss of the fob due to forgetfulness - *and the ability to start the car* - is higher.

A classic case of a solution in search of a problem.

Response leaders with clear objectives know better.

Remember the siren song of "we're not changing because we've always done it that way!"?

Well, sometimes they have a point. Evaluating proposed innovation through the following filters increases the probability that the new way may actually be better:

1. Does it solve a problem better, quicker or less expensively than the old way to solve the same problem?
2. Does it benefit a few people or a lot of people? (the impact of true innovation is usually widely felt)
3. Does the answer to WHAT and WHY have substance, or is the answer "just because we can"?

By applying a 'tad' of critical analysis to any proposed innovation, a Response Leader can improve their chances of riding the right horse off into the future.

Accomplishment

"A hero is born among a hundred, a wise man is found among a thousand, but an accomplished one might not be found even among a hundred thousand men." ~ Plato

---

Response leaders approach opportunities and challenges with one of two attitudes about achievement:

Static Attitude

This "fixed" attitude views accomplishment as a solid rock of success. To them:

- Everyone already has all of the intelligence and creativity they're going to get.
- They want to be a stabilizing force, work behind the scenes, etc.
- Any success must be hard fought and clutched tightly.
- They desire gradual, straight growth.
- They avoid any and all actions that may lead to failure.
- They will lead themselves just fine but are less likely to be interested in a visible role where they must lead others.
- They will more likely work for one organization for their whole career if they feel safe.
- They want freedom and sometimes isolation to do their job, not the pressure of advancement or leadership of others.
- They make excellent in-house experts.

Dynamic Attitude

A Dynamic or 'growth' attitude views accomplishment as an unlimited fountain of success from which to drink. To them:

- Success is a renewable resource.
- They want to change the world, be in charge, etc.

- Any success is merely a stopping point before their next success.
- They desire fast, upward growth.
- They see failure as an opportunity to begin again more intelligently.
- They will readily accept an opportunity where they can lead others to a common goal.
- They will more likely work for multiple organizations, all of which they will try to change for the better.
- They want new and challenging opportunities to learn.
- Their reward is in their efficient and creative effort.

(These findings are in part from research conducted by psychologist Carol Dweck.)

Response Leaders embracing a dynamic attitude hold an advantage over the static attitude.

For planned and unplanned events though, BOTH static and dynamic Response Leaders add value. Our job is to make sure that we cultivate the right attitude for the right role.

Static attitudes develop over time based on the feedback they receive after they succeed.

If a person (adult or child) gets constantly reinforced for being smart, being attractive or being a good teammate, they 'fix' into their mindset an attitude that believes that they only do well because they're smart, not because of their effort, which is dynamic.

To develop more dynamic leaders, change the feedback that you deliver.

- *Great effort!*
- *Super teamwork!*
- *Incredible problem-solving!*

It's important to remember that these are labels to aid in classifying behavior and leadership strategy.

A danger of overusing these labels is that confirmation bias may develop. That can lead to limiting a person's potential instead of cultivating it.

Once you learn and understand a person's tendency to have a static or a dynamic attitude, focus on the behavior, not the label.

Emotional Intelligence

"Minds without emotions are not really minds at all. They are souls on ice – cold, lifeless, creatures devoid of any desires, fears, sorrows, pains or pleasures." ~ Joseph E. LeDoux

---

Emotional Intelligence or EI is a field of study first pioneered by Daniel Goleman of Rutgers University. Since then, the field of EI has evolved and now defines the five primary emotions that comprise a Leader's emotional intelligence: Social skill, motivation, self-awareness, self-management, and empathy.

They each play a part in growing our Response Leader capacity so carefully review each component, below.

Social Skill

The popular 1990's TV show, Seinfeld, had a character, and I do mean character, named "Kramer." Kramer was known for bounding into his neighbor's apartment unannounced, speaking at will without filtering his comments, and hijacking any conversation to talk instead about his topic of choice.

On the show, Kramer was a hit. His character was very funny, very outlandish, and very memorable.

The Seinfeld show ran for nine years and enjoyed massive popularity. On a fictional sitcom, the character of Kramer worked exceptionally well and helped make the show an enduring favorite.

The Kramer character in a crisis? Not so much. Not because of his peculiar style or odd innovations but simply because he lacked the social grace and emotional intelligence to lead himself or others effectively.

With well-intentioned and well-honed social kills, Response Leaders are more likely to be effective in any size or type of group.

Motivation

Climbing Mount Kilimanjaro or rising at 5:00 a.m. every day to train for a marathon takes motivation. Leading oneself and others through a crisis also takes motivation.

Motivation is intrinsic and explains the reason why we exhibit certain behaviors. The behaviors of a person with an abundance of motivation will look much different than a person with little or no motivation.

As Response Leaders, these required, innate behaviors consist of things such as:

- Being among the first to arrive and among the last to leave when there's work to do.
- Willing to speak up and contribute when the need arises.
- Ready to make the gritty choice to pursue a difficult objective despite detractors, political pressure, or locust infestation.

Being disciplined, for example, to get to the job site early may produce a feeling of success in the near-term, but discipline alone often fails over the long-term. Motivation is the fuel that forms healthy habits, and healthy habits sustain a high level of Emotional Intelligence.

Motivated Response Leaders seldom start that way. Once they feel ownership of the organization's objectives and have the support of the people around them, however, there are few obstacles they are unwilling or un-motivated to overcome.

How to get and stay motivated is covered extensively in the topic, "The Wheel of Engagement™."

Awareness of Self

Response leaders are often also among the most influential people in a room. If they were to be ruffled, angry or apathetic, studies have shown that the others in the room will begin to 'mirror' those emotions.

Similarly, of course, if the Response Leader were to project an attitude of confidence (even if masking fear and uncertainty), the others will typically mirror those attitudes as well.

Confidence versus Courage

What's the difference between confidence and courage?

- **Courage** isn't fearlessness it's the willingness to press on even when afraid.
- **Confidence** is a belief your ability to accomplish the task at hand.

Having low confidence typically invites fear into our mind also. So, mustering a strong dose of courage can help us power through despite our fears or shaky confidence.

Being aware of oneself is a critical building block needed for a Response Leader to be emotionally intelligent.

Management of Self

One of the baseline assumptions of effective Response Leadership is the understanding that to effectively lead others, a Response Leader must lead themselves first.

And that starts with the regulation of an uncontrolled reaction to stress.

The amygdala is the part of the brain where anger, fear, impulse, and uncertainty is born. The amygdala will commandeer the part of the brain with waning confidence and force the bad decisions to start flowing if left unchecked.

Immediately stopping this hijacking attempt should involve a two-step intervention: Separate and breathe.

1.   **Separate** – Physically or at least mentally separate yourself from the rising tide of stress and the amygdala uprising.
2.   **Breathe** – Start with 3 and make sure they're deep and slow. Repeat.

Yes, there are fancier ways to stop the onslaught of a stress reaction. And if they work, you should use them.

In the spirit of simplicity, breathe and separate. Rinse-and-repeat again and again until you can effectively re-engage.

Empathy toward Others

Being empathetic is the ability for a Response Leader to think, feel or sense what the other person is experiencing.

Empathy may sound like a low priority option for a Response Leader to consider. However, it's one of the most important attitudes needed to earn trust, engagement, and support from the rest of the team.

Example:

Imagine Eileen delivering a briefing about new initiatives for the team that will commence immediately. She explains the reasons why the initiative has been adopted and includes a full breakdown of the functions impacted. She also includes a draconian new work schedule consisting of shorter lunches, weekend hours and canceled vacations.

Even with the team hearing and maybe even supporting the reason 'why' the initiative has been adopted, the direct and unapologetic impact to their individual work schedule is 'bad game.'

Even if considering the team's emotional satisfaction with the decision to adjust the work hours, Eileen's delivery lacked empathy and will erode not only her credibility but also the initiatives overall support.

In fact, if a Response Leader struggles or fails to accomplish their organization's objectives, a leading cause is because they did not incorporate an ingrained attitude of empathy for others into their approach to leadership.

In Eileen's case, taking a few moments before her meeting to note and evaluate the potential impact to the team and not just to her would go a long way in improving her empathy for others.

It's important to note that many times, delivering unpleasant news is a reality that all Response Leaders will eventually face. Being empathetic does not mean being evasive or soft.

Practicing and using finesse to empathetically acknowledge, consider and maybe even accommodate another person's experience is a hallmark of a world-class Response Leader.

Feedback

"Failure is only feedback. And feedback is a blessing." ~ Simon T. Bailey

---

In many circles, "feedback" is merely a nice term for tongue-lashing or brutal honesty. Therefore, the idea behind providing useful feedback is easier said than done.

"Great job!" or "Better luck next time!" is technically feedback but neither is particularly useful to do much besides to 'tweak' the ego.

Good feedback takes a tremendous amount of authenticity, a hallmark of a capable Response Leader.

When everyone is committed to accomplishing the objectives and in improving for future events, it becomes an honor to deliver and to receive feedback.

If your feedback is not well-received, evaluate your objectives and the feedback components below:

4 Components of Effective Feedback

Effective feedback has four parts:

WHY
WHEN
WHAT
HOW

WHY deliver the feedback.

All feedback should address a future, performance-based need.

- To confirm that the person giving the feedback observed the performance
- To improve future performances of the person receiving the feedback

Yet, we still hear this:

"I'm going to give you my brutally honest feedback."

Which is code for *"I am more interested in the brutality than I am in the honesty."*

Again, if your feedback isn't well-received, evaluate your objectives.

WHEN to deliver the feedback.

When is the best time to give feedback to your 3-year-old child who is about to run into a busy street?

a) Now.
b) Later.

When is the best time to deliver feedback to your colleague (who is currently in Aruba on vacation) who used poor punctuation in an interdepartmental email last week?

a) Now.
b) Later.

Timing may not be everything, but it's important.

Since your feedback is intended to help the recipient improve their performance, be sure to deliver your comments when it's the most likely to be well received - and acted upon - by the recipient.

- If appropriate, also consider asking the recipient for their preference.
- Perhaps they want it in writing, so they have a record of it instead of hearing it in-person
- Perhaps they want it on neutral ground, so they don't feel as defensive

- Perhaps they want it immediately, or maybe after everyone has a chance to sleep on it

Remember the objective of feedback is to improve the recipient's future performance.

WHAT type of feedback

- Behavior you want to repeat gets rewarded (positively reinforced)
- Behavior you do not want to repeat gets corrected (positively punished)

We can look to the dog world to see this in action:

1. Fido is required to sit before eating
   a. When he sits, he's told "Good Fido!" and permitted to eat
   b. Fido is therefore rewarded (positive reinforcement) by eating
   c. If this approach is consistent, Fido will be more likely to sit before eating in the future

2. Fido is not allowed on the couch
   a. Fido jumps on the couch anyway
   b. Fido is told "NO!" and if needed, physically removed from the couch (positive punishment)
   c. If this approach is consistent, Fido will be less likely to jump on the couch

3. Fido has to pee, so he goes on the carpet
   a. Fido is told "No!" and is shown the door to the backyard
   b. Fido is told "Good!" when he goes outside
   c. If this approach is consistent, when Fido has to pee sometime in the future he will more likely go to the door instead of peeing on the rug (negative reinforcement).

While improving the performance of a dog isn't quite as complicated as enhancing the performance of a human it doesn't have to be difficult either.

Not surprisingly, it starts with clear objectives.

If the recipient is expecting to hear how to improve how they assemble widgets, then focusing your feedback on how they drive a car is not going to produce results for either of you.

To improve a recipient's performance of a tactic or a strategy, focus on these types of feedback:

Feedback on a BEHAVIOR

It is common – because it's easy – to provide feedback on someone' personality. It's also petty and divisive.

To seek improvement, be sure to narrow the feedback down to specific behaviors and skip the commentary on their personality.

Example:

"Your personality is annoying."

vs.

"When you interrupt the speaker before they finish speaking, it makes it difficult to build trust among the team."

Remember, behavior that gets rewarded is likely to increase in both intensity and duration.

Feedback on a TACTIC

Tactics usually produce results that are black and white, yes or no, right or wrong. Delivering feedback on a tactic follows these general guidelines:

1. Reinforce their effort.
2. Validate the task to ensure you are both talking about the same thing.
3. Reinforce what part of the task they did well.
4. Isolate what part of the task they need to improve.
5. Offer to remove obstacles.

6. Offer to provide support.
7. Give them specific improvement instructions.
8. Reinforce their effort.

Example:

John's task was to put the following numbers in sequential order: "3 7 1 4 9 2."

John's efforts resulted in: "1 2 3 7 9 4."

Feedback to John might be: "This was a good effort. Your task was to put the numbers in sequential order. You were spot on with the first three numbers, but then you put the 4 at the end instead of after the 3. You have performed this task successfully before so checking your work should prevent the same mistake. Were they any other challenges you had where I can help you? Now let's try that again but check your work more carefully this time, okay? Thanks again for your effort."

Feedback on a STRATEGY

Strategies usually produce results that reflect the process used. The feedback, therefore, tends to be more interpretive between the person giving the feedback and the recipient. Delivering feedback on a strategy follows these general guidelines:

1. Acknowledge or thank the effort.
2. Validate the objective to ensure you are both talking about the same thing.
3. Identify the strategy used and the results achieved.
4. Challenge the recipient to provide alternatives to the current strategy.
5. Discuss the alternative outcomes and how they measure up against the objectives.
6. Offer to remove obstacles.
7. Offer to provide support.
8. Instruct them on how to use a better strategy to achieve better results.
9. Acknowledge or thank the effort.

Example:

Sally is assigned to the Logistics Section for the upcoming parade and received a request for 100 traffic cones for the upcoming parade.

Strategy: Sally called the local big box retailer and learned that they are $10 each. She used her issued credit card and paid $1000 for 100 cones.

Feedback to Sally might be: "Thanks for the effort you put into ordering the cones. Your objective was to obtain 100 cones. The strategy you used was to pay retail for them, which you did at a cost to this organization of $1000. Do you think there were other ways to have obtained 100 traffic cones? With a little coaching, Sally might suggest renting them from a vendor, getting bids from several vendors or requesting them from the city where the parade is scheduled to occur. If you had obtained them from the city at no cost, would that have allowed us to support the objective to be within our budget for the parade? Are there or were there any other obstacles to using this strategy where I can help you? In the future please always refer to the objectives before formulating and implementing your strategy, okay? Thanks for the effort you put into ordering the cones.

Other considerations for giving feedback:

- When or if there is an attempt by Sally to defer the project back to you, ask "what does your best judgment tell you to do?"
- We can only do what we are trained to do. Therefore, ensure that the feedback recipient receives training on the task or strategy before they are held responsible for any shortcomings!
- When/if the recipient pushes back, role play the result as if their strategy or tactics were correct. By illuminating their result, they'll more likely see why it needed improvement.
- You'll notice that any praise or acknowledgment of their effort did not directly precede the new instruction. Often, by giving too much praise before the suggested improvement, people will attach their focus to the praise but not what follows.

Remember, the purpose of all feedback is to improve the future performance!

HOW to give (and receive) feedback

Providing useful feedback involves a careful blend of confrontation and compassion.

With too much compassion the point gets lost in a sea of niceties, and the current level of performance continues or degrades.

- Being too friendly or empathetic, not wanting to come across as combative.

With too much confrontation the point gets lost in a jungle of thorny bushes, and the current level of performance continues or degrades.

- Being too harsh or "brutally honest" and forcing the recipient to fight back defensively.

In either case, the point gets lost.

Predictably, communicating clear and understandable objectives helps people connect to the mission.

- When people become connected to the mission, they are more likely to care about the mission.
- When people care, they are more likely to have compassion.
- When people become connected to the mission, they are more willing to confront others who are not supporting the mission.
- When people have compassion for others AND become connected to the mission, they are more likely to deliver balanced and useful feedback.

Before confronting a recipient with feedback that may be unpleasant or tense, ponder a few scenarios of how it might go first.

Plan and role play your response if the recipient becomes upset or angry and adjust your strategy accordingly.

Obviously, potentially difficult to receive feedback should be delivered in private to not exacerbate the recipient's potential feelings of embarrassment or inadequacy.

How Feedback is Rewarding

It should be clear by now that accomplishing the objectives that were set initially has its rewards.

Along the way, there may be opportunities to use rewards to strengthen the commitment to those objectives.

Rewarding the team for overall accomplishment: The sales TEAM earned the business - they ALL get rewarded equally.

Rewarding the individual for specific extra effort: Sally worked on the proposal late at night and early in the morning - she gets an INDIVIDUAL reward.

Remember, feedback is a 2-way street.

Reinforcing a culture of 2-way feedback is critical for high-performing teams.

- Well-managed organizations use supervisors to review the performance of subordinates and dispense feedback
- Well-led organizations use supervisors to evaluate the performance of subordinates and dispense feedback AND use subordinates to review the performance of supervisors and dispense feedback

I'm not talking about the antiquated once-per-year employee performance review scheme (well-established that they do not improve anyone's performance) either.

Authentic feedback is the hallmark of world-class Response Leadership.

Humility

"Pride is concerned with who is right. Humility is concerned with what is right." ~ *Ezra Taft Benson*

Some of the most toxic people in any given organization have several things in common.

One of them is their unbridled arrogance.

Or to put it more diplomatically, their lack of humility.

We've seen them, worked with them and maybe had even fallen victim to their bloated egos. While some may rise to elevated positions in their organization, they assuredly leave a wake of bruised and battered colleagues.

The humble Response Leader, on the other hand, understands that all significant accomplishments are the result of a team that is all pulling in the same direction.

They use:

> *"We"* instead of *"me."*
> *"Us"* instead of *"I."*

They measure their leadership against the short-term priorities and the long-term strategies of not just the event but the organization as a whole.

When it's time to take credit, they pass it around. When it's time to take the blame, humble Response Leaders shoulder it themselves and then privately coach anyone else who may have had a role.

At no time does a humble Response Leader expect their subordinate to be like them. They encourage individual growth and expression.

Response leaders exhibit humility at all times not just because it's what they do, but also because it's who they are.

Teams sometimes get enamored with arrogant 'leaders,' but true teams are only loyal to humble ones.

What Type of Leader are You?

Types of Leaders

"The questions we ask ourselves determine the type of people we will become." ~ Leo Babauta

---

Labels are good for knowing if you're about to accidentally sprinkle salt instead of sugar on your cobbler, but not so good for describing people.

Labels on people are sometimes restrictive, inconclusive, and demeaning.

There are some helpful exceptions though. To solidify our leadership capacity, evaluating the characteristics and tendencies of the behavior associated with a particular leadership type guides us and others how best to interact with them.

For example, if you know that a leader you are reporting to is 'all about' the command and control aspect of their position, then your strategy in dealing with them should be different than if they were more of a laissez-faire leader.

Let's break down some leadership types by, yes, labeling them by their characteristics. Many leaders will embody more than one style, too. They'll tap into the style that works for them depending on the situation at hand.

Therefore, I encourage you to study all of them and consider taking the best part of each one to add to your growing Response Leader duffel bag.

Servant Leader

Servant leadership is very popular these days. A recently promoted fire chief proudly told me recently that he was now a servant leader, and that at fire scenes he now stays "in the rear with the gear" in case there is a need for him to be a servant for his Captains fighting the fire 'up front.'

Similarly, when Jimmy Carter was elected President of the United States in 1976, he saw himself as a servant leader before the term became popular. He went as far as insisting that he carry his luggage into the white house on move-in day, in full view of the press corps who widely broadcast and reported the new president's selfless act of 'servitude.'

Except that it backfired. It took quite awhile for President Carter to earn the respect of many American's and many elected politicians in the USA and abroad. Many believe it is because he chose to focus more on being a servant rather than being a service-oriented leader. There is a distinction, and it often makes the difference between being effective as a leader and being ineffective.

I'm not a big fan of the common portrayal of servant leadership. Good leadership is not about servitude; it's about service.

Example:

During our response to Hurricane Katrina in New Orleans, our Response Leaders faced a daunting task: lead us into *and safely out of* those horrific conditions while helping as many people as possible. They were unwavering in their focus, relentless in their expectations and supportive of our efforts. One of our hardened and steadfast leaders started out each day bringing us each a cup of hot coffee, a smile, and an encouraging word to our tent every morning. He didn't have to serve us coffee with a smile, yet his selfless service helped us 'get our head right' about the tasks that lay ahead.

His actions provide a simple but effective example of service-oriented leadership.

Command and Control Leader

You've also heard this kind of leader referred to as an autocratic, coercive, or authoritative leader.

The image people conjure of a command and control leader is a uniformed officer pounding their fist on the table and yelling directions at their subordinates while they huddle in fear.

While that may be true, there are also many times when we need someone with absolute authority and the presence to command and control an environment.

For example, if the ship is sinking, the captain that will save the most lives is the one unapologetically barking evacuation instructions to the crew.

However, that same style of leadership is not a good fit when the captain is coaching his kid's Little League game on the weekend.

Therefore, a little bit of command and control goes a long way.

Note: modern incident managers often modify this leadership label from "command and control" to "command and manage."

Democratic Leader

Democratic leaders tend to give everyone a voice to share their opinion. This all-hands approach can do wonders for engagement and participation since more people feel that they have a say in what happens next.

The downside is that 'group-sourcing' decisions can take a great deal of time before making a decision.

Charismatic Leader

The charismatic leader boosts morale and is often their organization's number one cheerleader.

This style is ideal when a happy face is needed to represent the organization, like Virgin Group founder, Richard Branson.

Charismatic leaders are seen on stage leading the pep rally and inspiring new initiatives. Their downfall is when, particularly during a crisis, they attempt to be serious, which may appear to be forced and lacking in authenticity.

Laissez-Faire Leader

This leader is fond of saying "it will work out" without having a plan for it to work out. Of course, when it works out it's because someone was decidedly not laissez-faire about it and took care of business.

Acting in a hands-off, non-intervening way can often be helpful for a leader, but being absent too often isn't leadership, it's called a vacation.

The good news is that behind the behaviors that define the different leadership types, they are all just labels. And labels do not define how effective we are as Response Leaders.

In fact, the most successful leaders tend to embody several styles of leadership and rely on the most appropriate style based on the situation at hand.

An example is very well-known military leader James Mattis. He has demonstrated proficiency in many of the different leadership types, but only one at a time, depending on the situation.

An example, in his own words:

"America has two fundamental powers. One is the power of intimidation. I was part of it and America will defend herself and our idea, this experiment that we call America. And that's all it is, is an experiment in democracy. But the other power I think that perhaps we have used less in recent years, last 20 years maybe, is the power of inspiration. And I think that the power of inspiration of America at times has got to be employed just as strongly." ~ Retired Marine Gen. James Mattis

---

Transformational and Transactional Leaders

Response leaders always have their eye on the prize. And by the prize, I mean the result of accomplishing the mission priorities and objectives.

Example:

Say the objective is to go to a parlor to get ice cream.

Even in the face of road closures, screaming kids and an impending kick-off of their favorite team's game, the Response Leader always has a mental image of what it will be like to slurp up some Rocky Road ice cream.

It takes practice to refine the mental images, but when what we imagine becomes real, it's all worth it.

By sharing those images and bringing the mission to life for others, a Response Leader can become transformational.

Transformational Leader – helping people transform from their current condition to a better condition.

You'll hear them also referred to as change agents, coaches, and mentors.

"If you want to build a ship, don't herd people together to collect wood and don't assign them tasks and work, but rather teach them to long for the endless immensity of the sea." ~ Antoine de Saint-Exupéry

---

Transforming can lead to an ideal state, but there's an evil twin of the transformational leader called a transactional leader.

Transactional Leader – leading someone based on specific, short-term tasks.

Example:

Instead of helping them envision the cool taste of ice-cream despite any obstacle, transactional leaders focus instead on managing the task of driving in traffic, of getting home before the game starts, of suppressing the kid's outbursts, etc.

- Transactional leaders focus on what's measured, i.e., time in traffic, quiet versus noisy children, etc.

- Transformational leaders focus on the future condition, i.e., growth, strategy, and vision.

Perhaps the definitions were helpful, but they hardly matter.

What is important is that the Response Leader understands what results they should expect when they're transactional versus when they're transformational.

Here's another more salient example of the Response Leader who's approaching their work as a series of transactions and the actual outcome they create:

The Browerville Fire Department has 24 stations so far in service to their growing community. The Browerville Chief has been under pressure by the city manager to maintain and in some cases lower costs to maximize the funds available for the city's growth initiatives.

During the chief's regular visits to each station, the chief makes a point to address and question:

1. The extra medical training supplies consumed
2. The water bill being higher than normal
3. The overtime paid to some of the firefighters

The captains explain that:

1. The extra training supplies were to address a noted deficiency in some of the medic's bandaging skills by doing some in-service training
2. The higher water bill was because of the extra washing of the fire apparatus so that they are clean during the increased visits by the public and local politicians (including the city manager)
3. The overtime was used to help mentor junior officers so that they'll be ready to promote when the number of fire stations expands

The chief doubles-down on the cost-cutting and demands that they do more with less. The chief requires the delivery of daily reports to his office for overtime, training supplies, and water usage by noon each day for review and feedback.

The firefighters begin to lose trust that the chief has their best interests in mind. The resentment they feel toward the chief continues to grow, and the productivity increases that the chief demanded begins to decrease.

1. Productivity is low.
2. Morale is low.
3. The Browerville Fire Department is in turmoil and becomes one of the last city departments to receive budget consideration.

The chief's extreme focus on productivity has created three (3) party fouls common to transactional leaders:

1. Micromanagement
2. Lack of vision
3. Too much focus on productivity

The story helps to frame how those fouls can appear slowly but can grow until the ripping fibers of the organization can be heard a mile away.

The unfortunate reality is that while the execution failed, the intent may likely be valid:

- Large and growing organizations need managing, just not micro-managing.
- Near-term vision can also help sustain the long-term vision.
- Productivity that gets measured can also be productivity that gets funded.

Let's look at some root-causes:

Perhaps the chief was ill-equipped to be a better advocate for their department in budget meetings?

Perhaps the chief was also personally burdened with having to provide consistent evidence of productivity?

Perhaps the leadership environment in the whole city has inadvertently fostered a transactional approach?

Except for a few notable exceptions, most people don't intend to perform poorly at their job.

However, it's also quite easy to overlook and accidentally reinforce some of these subtle, destructive behaviors until they bubble to the surface.

Possible Solutions:

1. Assessing the path that these transactions took can help find the root.
2. After unearthing the source of this transactional approach, seek to understand the WHAT and the WHY of this method.
3. Suggest a combined effort to transform the WHAT and the WHY into objectives that everyone can get behind.
4. Become an active leader in the transformation from the WHAT and the WHY to the result that everyone supports.

Integrity and Ethics

"If you have integrity, nothing else matters. If you don't have integrity, nothing else matters." ~Alan Simpson

---

Personally, I've always been perplexed by the presence of ethics courses in college and in business whose aim is to educate folks how to be moral and honest.

Unlike the much more eloquent quote above, I associate integrity to being pregnant; either you are, or you are not. Just like people are ethical or they're not.

Nonetheless, integrity (morals) and ethics (actions) are part of the glue that holds the rest of the Response Leader's mindset together.

Example:

Rick is innovative, calm under pressure and accomplished in his role. Most would say that he has the traits and the followership of a bona fide leader. He also has the authority and the funding that go with those accomplishments. With that authority and funding, Rick also discovered that he has less oversight than most people in the organization. As he dutifully moves those funds around to support the organization's mission, he's also found a way to siphon off some funds to support his family's mission to the Bahamas along with a new set of golf clubs. *Bad Rick.*

Leading without integrity isn't leading, it's manipulation and deceit.

Rick may have had some ethics training too. But it sure didn't stick, did it? And that's the folly of trying to mandate morality. It just doesn't work.

To improve ethical decision-making, comprehensive scenario-based and discussion-based exercises should occur.

So, while integrity is paramount to the current and future success of a Response Leader, if they (you) like to play it fast and loose with the truth, then there's nothing I can say here to convince you otherwise.

My kids have heard me preach many times: *"How you do one thing is how you do everything."*

When people have the mindset to do what is right, when it's right, they build their comfort in embracing that mindset all of the time, for every situation.

We are, quite simply, a sum of what we repeatedly do.

Priorities

"The best leaders satisfy multiple priorities with each activity. This actually enables them to increase their focus while reducing their number of actions." ~ *John C. Maxwell*

Priorities sit at the top of the decision-making tree.

- **Priorities** are *what you want*
- **Objectives** are *what you do to get what you want*
- **Strategies** are *how you do it*
- **Tactics** are *the actual doing*

In any other order, we lose sight of the big picture and end up digging a ditch in the backyard instead of planting a tree in the front yard.

As events scale in size and complexity, whether planned or unplanned, the demands on the Response Leader's attention increase as well.

Priorities provide the touchstone that the Response Leader can return to again and again to ensure that the ship is sailing in the right direction.

For unplanned events that endanger the public (disasters, etc.) I've found one phrase that keeps me grounded in the priority:

"Do the Most Good, For the Most People, in the Least Amount of Time with the Least Amount of Risk." ~ *Mike McKenna*

Response Leaders that commit themselves to "Do the Most Good, For the Most People, in the Least Amount of Time with the Least Amount of Risk" enjoy more satisfying outcomes.

Similarly, there's an acronym that helps make the point: L.I.P.S.

L*ife Safety* - protect yourself, your team and your victim in that order before anything else.

I*ncident Stabilization* - Stop the problem from worsening.

P*roperty Preservation* - Save property from further damage.

S*ocietal Restoration* - Bring the community back to pre-event condition.

Example:

The creek is rising and threatening the daycare facility. The priorities in order are to:

1. Evacuate the children and staff to a better place. (Life Safety)
2. Place barricades in the area to prevent motorists from driving into flood water. (Incident Stabilization)
3. Dam up the outside of the daycare with sandbags to reduce water damage to the building. (Property Preservation)
4. Clean up flood debris, remove sandbags, make repairs, and resume normal operations. (Societal Restoration)

There are other acronyms and mnemonics used to reference these response priorities; L.I.P.S. is just one of them.

Response leaders find a system of remembering and applying important concepts that work for them.

Continuous Improvement

"You will find that the mere resolve not to be useless, and the honest desire to help other people, will, in the quickest and delicatest ways, improve yourself." ~ John Ruskin

---

If you've ever trained a dog, you know that they're always learning something. Maybe it's that sit means sit.

Or maybe it's that if they beg long enough, they can make you give them a treat, pet them, or throw their ball.

You see, someone is always getting trained.

If your dog Fido can make you throw the ball for him when all you wanted to do is sit and read your horoscope then congratulations, YOU are the one getting trained.

The point is that all of us are always learning either the right way to do something or the wrong way to do something.

And what we learn accumulates into our performance, good or bad.

To conclude any event better, smarter, and faster than when we started, then we must embrace this learning dynamic sooner rather than later.

Later in this material, we'll discuss the specific parts and pieces of ending an event as an organization. However, evaluating our performance and the performance of our direct reports should be constant, ever-present, and authentically communicated.

Most innovative organizations have learned this and have finally abandoned the practice of annual reviews. They simply do a poor job of providing relevant feedback based on a year's worth of performance at one time.

By adopting the mindset that improvement is the sum of thousands of small acts and choices, Response Leaders can improve themselves and others on a continuous and consistent basis.

Delegation

"Surround yourself with the best people you can find, delegate authority, and don't interfere." ~ *Ronald Reagan*

Events are handled best at the lowest hierarchical level possible.

If we spill a cup of coffee, there's likely not a very good reason to call out the Army's National Guard to help clean it up.

On the other end of the spectrum, for an EF5 tornado that rips through a populated area, the Army's National Guard won't be nearly enough assistance.

The fundamental mindset here is to understand and appreciate the role of delegation.

In a functional based system like Response Leadership, the first person involved in the event after the 'trigger' is expected to perform every single task until the event ends.

Since that's impractical for most events, the initial Response Leader must start to delegate or assign functions and tasks to other Response Leaders to maintain momentum within The Response Leadership Sequence™.

The specifics of resource planning are covered in depth later.

Command Presence and Attitude

"When placed in command - take charge." ~ General Norman Schwarzkopf (Ret.)

A positive attitude is one that sees the potential in every challenge, not that everything always works out for the best.

There's research that suggests that merely adopting a power pose (hands on hips, shoulders back, head up, feet spaced shoulder width, etc.) can add as much as 25% to our confidence level.

The same applies to having a Command Presence.

Command Presence: stature and aura of confidence and strength.

- I've seen commanding and effective Response Leaders that are *bigger than life* that inspire everyone to sit up and take note when they speak.
- I've seen commanding and effective Response Leaders that are *quiet and unassuming* that inspire everyone to sit up and take note when they speak.

Here are some important notes on what I'm NOT saying:

I'm definitely NOT referring to the people who say *"Everything will work out!"* They're also the same people who do nothing about it, leaving the actual 'working it out' part to others. If I had a dollar for every instance that I have been around these types of people, I'd be wealthy.

- I'm not saying that confidence alone makes one a capable Response Leader.
- I'm not saying that having a commanding presence makes one a capable Response Leader.

While everyone's mileage will vary, confident Response Leaders that understand how to exhibit a Command Presence authentically are also usually capable Response Leaders.

Readiness to Act - Introduction

"Fairy tales do not tell children the dragons exist. Children already know that dragons exist. Fairy tales tell children the dragons can be killed." ~ Gilbert Chesterton

---

Preparedness and survival are a multi-billion-dollar industry in the United States with millions of people preparing themselves with hordes of contingencies for a doomsday type event.

Contingency planning - discussed separately - is certainly a hallmark of a Response Leader and being prepared with the right tools goes hand and hand.

Therefore, if a little preparedness is good, then a lot of preparedness should be very good, right?

Being a Response Leadership educator, I've encountered many, many people who are well-stocked for an emergency.

And that includes people that I've helped rescue and evacuate that had prepared, yet were paralyzed by the mistaken belief that the act of preparing was the same as preparing to act.

And therein lies the difference between someone with a closet full of supplies when disaster strikes and someone who is already uphill, upwind and out of harm's way.

I call it the **Readiness to Act**.

A person with an attitude that primes them to take action will survive a lot longer than a person huddled with a year's supply of canned beans.

The "it can't happen to me" attitude is how people end up in an OSHA case study so a Readiness to Act starts with the mental mindset that something unpleasant could in fact happen.

Once we accept that a bad thing can happen, then we can begin to frame our conscious and subconscious mind to envision what our part looks and feels like while responding to the bad thing.

By preparing ourselves mentally first, the case of beans, extra band-aids, and spare bullets gains relevancy.

Example:

- Ruth accepts that bad stuff happens, like an earthquake.
- Ruth envisions what that bad thing looks like in great detail. Sights, sounds, etc.
- Ruth also envisions in great detail what her response looks like, including what support she needs to respond successfully.
- Ruth replays this mental video as often as needed to gain comfort and confidence in the idea of responding for real.
- Ruth is mentally prepared. The mental video has become the default and has replaced fear and uncertainty.
- Ruth acquires the support she needs (more training, more tools, more supplies, etc.)
- Ruth is physically prepared.
- When or if the actual bad thing happens, Ruth has a Readiness to Act.
- Ruth is a Response Leader.
- Be like Ruth!

Response leaders can easily monitor and strengthen their Readiness to Act by scanning their mental video library for videos that match the scenario for which they're planning. If there's no current video, then repeat the steps above!

An entire, separate section will dig deeper into the Readiness to Act.

The Response Leadership Sequence ™ – Part 1

- Before the airline pilot takes to the friendly skies, they follow a sequence …
- Before the surgeon slices their patient open to remove their kidney, they follow a sequence …
- Before the virtuoso begins their symphony, they follow a sequence …

And before the Response Leader conquers an event, they follow a sequence.

The Response Leadership Sequence™ addresses the universal steps in the life cycle of a successful event.

The right mindset enables the Response Leader to approach any crisis with competence and clarity. That's why the foundation of the sequence starts with mindset.

Having an adequate mindset is the one area of a crisis where we have absolute control and why I dedicate a prior section to discussing the Response Leader Mindset.

The remaining phases of The Response Leadership Sequence™ each have outside forces that can influence the outcome. Therefore, maintaining a strong and accessible foundation of mental models or "rules for living" is useful.

Five Phases of The Response Leadership Sequence™

Some events are planned (like a sporting event), and some are unplanned (like a cyber-attack).

Some events are small (like a bake sale), and some are large (like a multi-site special event).

Some are resolved quickly by one or two people (like a fire in the copier room), and some are long in duration that requires the services of many (like the impact from a hurricane).

All successful responses start with Response Leaders having a successful mindset.

- They each require a Readiness to Act, which is the product of focused planning.
- Every event has a planned or unplanned trigger that kicks-off the response.
- Each event has a clear and competently managed response.
- They all conclude successfully with a satisfying resolution.

Therefore, the flow of the five major phases of The Response Leadership Sequence ™ is:

1. **Leader's Mindset**
2. **Readiness to Act**
3. **Response Trigger**
4. **Response Leadership**
5. **Response Resolution**

Understanding The Response Leadership Sequence™ is the first step the Response Leader needs to know to smartly begin, efficiently lead and effectively end any and all responses.

However, before the event can end successfully, it has to have a beginning.

Let's get packed.

Leadership Readiness to Act and Their D.U.F.F.E.L. B.A.G.

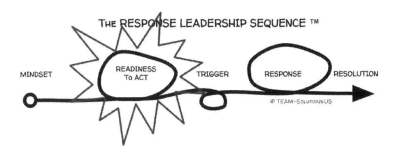

Leaders prepare, responders, take action.

However, Response Leaders build and maintain a Readiness to Act.

The Readiness to Act is illustrated using a standard duffel bag.

Duffel bags are ideal for carrying tools and resources we need to prepare for a planned or unplanned event.

For the Response Leader, their duffel bag consists of the following actionable skills, expressed as their D.U.F.F.E.L. B.A.G.:

1. Developing
2. Unifying
3. Forecasting
4. Funding
5. Equipping
6. Learning
7. Boosting
8. Assessing
9. Getting Ready to Act

D.U.F.F.E.L. B.A.G.

Memorizing the mnemonic is not nearly as important as knowing, understanding and implementing each action-oriented phase.

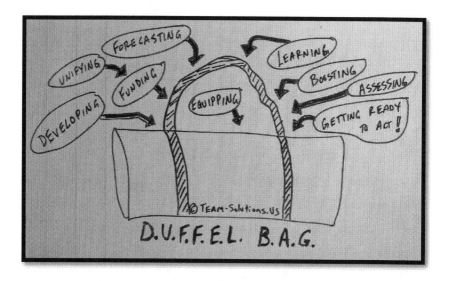

Let's begin.

Developing the Plan

Your D.U.F.F.E.L. B.A.G.:

1. *Developing*
2. Unifying
3. Forecasting
4. Funding
5. Equipping
6. Learning
7. Boosting
8. Assessing
9. Getting Ready to Act

"If you are going to achieve excellence in big things, you develop the habit in little matters. Excellence is not an exception; it is a prevailing attitude." ~ Colin Powell

---

For an event plan to be successful, answer two (2) questions first.

These two questions are typically answered by whoever is in the organization's leadership (CEO, Board of Directors, Executive Director, etc.) with the inspiration, the responsibility or the authority to host a planned event or to respond to an event that's unplanned.

However, many places within an organization also require the leadership to initiate an event plan:

- Perhaps the idea is conceived at the department level by the IT director who wants to be able to lead a combined response to a cyber-attack ...
- Perhaps the idea is generated by a volunteer responder who wants to make their team more relevant and utilized.

Regardless where the Response Leader sits within the organization, the foundation for a sustainable plan all starts with a solid foundation.

And the more solid the foundation, the more that you can build on top of it.

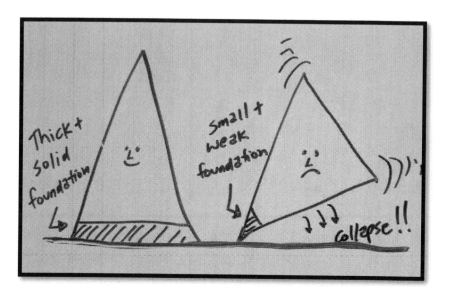

The 2 Answers To Answer First

1. *WHAT* do you want to accomplish?

What's the mission? What's the leader's intent? What are the strategic decisions?

Knowing the desired outcome is always the first step. It doesn't need to be overly precise, but it does need to communicate a large enough target to shoot.

WHAT Examples:

- Host a fundraising tournament.
- Enjoy a family vacation to Disney World.
- Recover from a disruption of any kind.
- Grow an authentic and organized business.

2. *WHY* are you wanting or needing to accomplish this?

> *To create an informed crisis response plan?*
> *To meet budget requirements for an annual fundraiser?*
> *To be resilient in case of a business interruption?*

Answering "WHY" is what transforms the project into a mission.

And missions are a needed ingredient to engage and inspire the entire organization to participate enthusiastically.

Take the "WHAT" answer and add "... in order to ...." to the end. That becomes your "WHY."

WHY Examples:

- Host a fundraising tournament ... in order to ... raise enough money to sustain and grow the organization for a full year, pay for a trip to Rome, feed hungry kids, etc.
- Enjoy a family vacation to Disney World ... in order to ... bond as a family through shared adventures, etc.
- Recover from a disruption of any kind ... in order to ... maintain viable patient care, staff employment, etc.

- Grow an authentic and organized business … in order to … provide for my family, serve others, successfully model best-practices to my kids, etc.

One of the most helpful forms that the Incident Command System (ICS) offers us is the ICS 201 Incident Briefing.

An entire upcoming section is dedicated to ICS forms and how they assist us.

When the ICS 201 filled out, it captures almost all of the critical building blocks needed to start an event off on the right foot. It includes things like:

- Map
- Summary
- Objectives
- Organizational structure
- Safety concerns
- Current actions
- Available resources

Many events that are short in duration and not very dynamic or that don't require lots of resources may not even extend beyond the use of an ICS 201.

The conventional practice is that any incident that goes beyond one operational period - usually 12 or 24 hours - will need a completed Incident Action Plan (IAP) which is a book of completed ICS forms.

I provide a more thorough explanation of operational periods, requesting additional resources, and action plans in an upcoming section.

WHAT and *WHY.*

The first two pillars of successful Response Leadership and the initial draft of what will be our event's strategic objectives.

Decision-Making Methods

"No sensible decision can be made any longer without taking into account not only the world as it is but the world as it will be ..." ~ Isaac Asimov

---

If making a good decision was easy, everyone would be doing it, right?

Different people naturally rely on different decision-making methods, but Response Leaders reply on 'next-level' thinking and an entire tool-bag of methods.

The below methods are not all-inclusive nor are they mandatory. However, in my research of successful Response Leaders, these represent some of the most prevalent and useful.

"Long-range planning does not deal with future decisions, but with the future of present decisions." ~ Peter Drucker

---

Next-Level Thinking

"The players are healthy, and they're playing at home. Therefore we should win the game."

Maybe, but even though that belief is easy to defend, it's also overly simplistic.

Next-level thinking requires looking past the initial decision and asking the deep questions.

In dealing with others, we can ask "why do you think that?" or other next-level question to peel back the reasoning.

To guard against our first-level thinking, we can ask ourselves:

- *What's the chance I'm right?*
- *What could go wrong?*
- *What other outcomes are possible?*
- *What happens next?*

The best results come from the best decisions, and the best decisions come from next-level thinking.

Let's look more closely at some other decision-making tools. Many can benefit you collectively or independently.

Just like with our mental models, these decision-making tools must be brought to the forefront of our thinking by practice, considered thought and confident execution.

Criteria-Based Decision-Making

The inconvenient reality is that in the real-world our decisions don't result in a buzzer and flashing light that tells us that we're right or wrong (that's what parents and teachers are for!)

The real-world does give us expected and definitive outcomes, however.

Decision: *eat an entire jar of tabasco peppers*
Expected Outcome: *heartburn*

Decision: *allow untrained people into a disaster environment*
Expected Outcome: *injury and liability*

On the surface, those decisions may seem justifiable. But by pulling back the layers to examine the criteria used to make each decision, we can learn that the decision-making criteria was deficient.

Instead of focusing only on the decision's desired outcome, consider putting greater effort into the criteria used to decide the first place.

For example, Tim's Tech is a computer parts and supply store with some limited repair services available. Tim, the owner, wants to increase profit, so he decides to start offering house calls to repair home computers and home networks.

Criteria: Motivated by the outcome, Tim sees other stores offering in-home service and assumes they are profitable as a result
Decision: Offer in-home service to his customers
Expected Outcome: Increased profit

After he informs his staff, they argue about the increased burden of only the existing personnel providing in-home service and concerns that their schedules will be forced to change to accommodate night and weekend service hours. In short, they are not supportive of Tim's decision because it was focused too narrowly on the outcome.

After the pushback, he invites his staff to join him in making the decision. Tim's objective? Make more profit.

They start by looking closely at the criteria.

- By doing a little research, they discover that the other stores offering in-home service are forced to endure high insurance rates, high turnover and little demand for the service. In short, their net profit is lower.

- Tim's staff looked next at their existing services. By deciding to add just two hours per day to their business hours they can service a larger customer base. Those customers can then drop off their computers before or after work for repair whereby the previous hours conflicted.

- The staff also decided to publicize a telephone number for existing customers to call into the shop for phone support for their home network.

By focusing more on the criteria to make their decision instead of just the outcome, Tim's Tech decision about what to do next essentially made itself.

Agreeing or disagreeing about the decision-making criteria instead of just the outcome will enrich the process and ultimately improve the outcome.

Using sensible criteria also creates an "If This, Then That" formula that paves the way to better decisions. And since good decisions usually turn into good results, the whole process becomes meritocratic.

Remember, Response Leaders that embrace merit-based processes can build upon their successes, which is good for everyone.

To confidently arrive at the What and the Why of crisis decision-making, use one or more of the following decision-making methods.

A summary of all decision-making models is at the end of this section.

Concrete, Abstract, Sequential & Random Decisions

1. **Concrete Decision-Making** - relies on all available details and analysis.
2. **Abstract Decision-Making** - relies on analysis and theory from relevant data.
3. **Sequential Decision-Making** - relies on data in step-by-step, logical progression.
4. **Random Decision-Making** - relies on impulse and random thinking.

Example:

Bob's Burger Barn wants to expand their services to include chicken (WHAT) to appeal to a wider range of customer (WHY). Bob, the owner, has given the team the task to decide if it's a viable option.

Sam says: *"Out of the 100% of mouths that eat out in this community, we could increase our 20% to at least 30% simply by increasing the size of our chicken selections."* Sam is a **Concrete decision-maker**.

Sally says: *"Since cow meat is less healthy and chicken meat is healthier, more people will eventually eat more chicken."* Sally is an **Abstract decision-maker**.

Bill says: *"In the last five years, wholesalers sold more chickens than cows to restaurants. The wholesale price of chicken has gone down, but the retail price has gone up. Conversely, the wholesale price of beef has gone up, but the retail price has not. Therefore, the profit is greater in serving chicken versus serving beef."* Bill is a **Sequential decision-maker**.

Beth says: *"More cows are characterized on TV with names and personalities than chickens, so people are more likely to eat a dead chicken rather than a dead cow."* Bill is a **Random decision-maker**.

Please note that I have no clue if any of those data points are accurate or not. I present them for comparative purposes only. If you are a cattle rancher who makes your living selling beef to restaurants, no disparagement was intended!

How it helps you: When assembling key decision-makers, a mix of the above thinking styles will add more value than just one or two.

Other notable decision-making tactics will also aid in quality outcomes for the Response Leader.

High-Speed Decisions v. Analysis Paralysis

High-quality decisions have impact, relevance and are far-reaching.

- *Buying a house?*
- *Marrying your love interest?*
- *Announcing the debut of "New Coke?"*
- *Evacuating a building?*
- *Requesting help from the governor?*

Even seasoned Response Leaders need to ruminate over those topics before deciding what to do and when.

But will the decision still be impactful, relevant and far-reaching if the decision-maker lingers too long before actually making the decision?

A common stumbling block is a sort of 'analysis paralysis,' or being stuck in a circle of never-ending delays, negotiations, and excessive research.

- *What if ghosts haunt the house?*
- *What if she says no?*
- *What if everybody misses the original Coke?*
- *What if the threat wasn't real?*
- *What if I embarrass myself?*

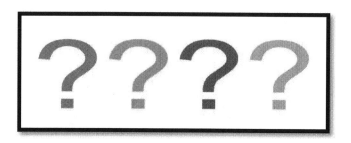

Overall, *what if I make a bad choice?*

The 'What If' game works well for contingency planning (discussed later) but can sabotage the benefits of a speedy and meaningful decision.

A study conducted by the Journal of Consumer Research identified 'choice closure' as a successful tactic to move on after making a decision.

In their study, researchers evaluated diners at a restaurant comparing those who quickly closed their menu after ordering with those that kept their menu open and repeatedly reconsidered their menu choice. After eating, the researchers surveyed the diners on their level of satisfaction with their food choice and not surprisingly, the diners that kept circling back to evaluate their options, again and again, reported a much lower level of satisfaction than those that simply closed their menu after making their initial choice.

Matched with a high-quality decision, making a speedy choice seems like a home-run, right?

How it helps you: The implication is that high-quality and high-speed decisions are the way to go, but as Response Leaders, we must carefully evaluate and predict which tactics will produce the best outcomes.

We'll cover the impediments and considerations to these high-quality and high-speed decisions more thoroughly in a moment.

Your refined mental models come in handy here, too. By considering the impact of your cognitive biases, for example, you can reduce or eliminate them to make more efficient decisions.

Reversible Decisions v. Non-Reversible Decisions

Some outcomes from our decisions are more consequential than others.

Decisions that **are not** reversible require great consideration and forethought before making them.

Examples:

- Naming your child 'Apostrophe.'
- Tearing the damaged building down after assuming no more victims are inside.

Decisions that **are** reversible are also changeable if the outcome doesn't measure up.

Examples:

- Buying the green leisure suit with the wide lapel
- Sending resources to the 3rd floor versus the 2nd floor

If a decision is not reversible, consider the risks more thoroughly first.

If a decision is reversible, make it quickly.

How it helps you: By determining the lasting effect your decision will have, you can speed up or slow down the process.

Automated Decisions

Some decisions can be automated. And if they 'can' be automated, Response Leaders must also evaluate whether they 'should' be automated.

The benefits of automated decision-making can be significant. When properly applied, leaders gain two elusive advantages:

1. **More Time**
2. **More Productivity**

For example, imagine if you decided that for one full week you would automate some of the more mundane or routine decisions in your day:

- You would decide in advance to automate your food choices for every meal, i.e., oatmeal every morning, a tuna sandwich for every lunch and beans and rice for every dinner.
- You would decide in advance to automate the process of getting dressed by wearing the same 'uniform' every day.
- You would decide in advance to automate the care and upkeep of your yard to a professional landscaper.
- You would decide to automate your technical decisions to a delegate (like updating your website, repairing your vehicle or auto-replying to some emails).

Even at 30 minutes per day of saved time and mental energy, at the end of the 7-day period, you have reclaimed 3.5 hours of time and brain power to apply elsewhere. What could you do with 3.5 of extra time and brainpower per week?

On the one hand, it sounds very institutional, but the advantages are obvious. Better decisions, in this case, automated decisions, give leaders the extra time and energy to apply to more consequential activities, like leading with clarity and competence.

Automation for the home and office is increasingly available and is another example of the freeing effects of removing mundane or routine decisions. Even something as simple as automatically controlling your lights, temperature, and coffee-maker every day (automated decision-making), little bits of time return to your family and workforce.

The rise of subscription services is another excellent example of automation used for good. Instead of needing to remember things like replacing toothbrushes, backfilling paper towels, and updating your website software, a subscription service decides and takes action for us. In turn, we have increased the mental space to focus on more noteworthy decisions.

1. **More Time**
2. **More Productivity**

Standing orders are another example of automated decision-making:

- Like in the old spaghetti westerns: *"when you see the whites of their eyes, shoot!"*
- Or Young Billy, in the midst of swiping some cookies off the counter, demands that his sister Little Ruthie *"tell me when you hear Mom coming!"*
- Or, *"when the water level rises beyond that line, evacuate everybody to the rally point."*

Standing orders are control-oriented decisions that remove the need for the decision-maker to do anything except take action on a specific stimulus.

While standing orders have some utility during a crisis, they do little to empower others to make independent choices. Independent decision-makers are usually desirable over those reliant on a higher authority.

The desired outcome of automated decision-making before, during and after a crisis is to reduce the number of decisions made, so that time and energy are available to spend elsewhere.

If an automated decision creates more work or takes more time to manage, then it should be re-evaluated.

How it helps you: When automating more decisions, you are liberated to focus on more consequential activities.

Computational Decision-Making

Imagine you're performing an online search for a new travel bag and travel deals for Rome. Immediately afterward you start seeing advertisements for travel accessories, travel booking sites, and things-to-do-while-in-Rome sites.

The savvy marketers are taking advantage of the benefits of algorithms, or computational decision-making to predict a behavioral sequence:

1. Sam shops for a travel bag and cheap flights to Rome.
2. That pattern predicts an upcoming trip.
3. Similar trip planners also search for itinerary services, a place to stay, travel insurance, etc.
4. Instead of displaying ads for lawn mowers, you see ads for these travel related services and products.

The gremlins inside your computer are programmed to look for patterns and sequences to serve up those offers from advertisers.

A service to some, an aggravation to others, but a lesson for us all.

Being able to identify patterns and sequences can provide a Response Leader with powerful decision-making skills.

Now imagine you're a Response Leader at the Acme Call Center located near the Gulf of Mexico during hurricane season.

1. Weather reports indicate a rapidly developing tropical disturbance offshore headed your way.
2. Communities, organizations, and families that find themselves in this environment have a limited time to evacuate, execute their robust sheltering plan, or implement other severe weather procedures.
3. In other words, there's a predictable pattern and sequence to what does and should occur before landfall, all based on the input from the weather reports.
4. At 96-hours pre-landfall, this happens. At 24-hours pre-landfall, that happens.

Evacuating your facility when there's no threat is usually an unsavory decision but taking decisive action based on the patterns and sequences of a hurricane can save lives.

A quality output from a computational decision requires quality input. Therefore, unless the Response Leader is receiving adequate situational awareness to support their decision, the quality of the decision they deliver will be diminished, sometimes drastically.

How it helps you: By identifying patterns, you can start to get ahead of the crisis instead of operating 'behind the curve.'

Technical or Process-Oriented Decisions

These are the nuanced decisions that define our productivity.

In a governmental office, a technical decision may be an information management process that feeds data into a document archive. While many leaders are responsible for the compliance of those procedures, they can usually delegate the approval and automate the reporting. More on delegation later.

Unfortunately, like an assembly line, many technical or process-oriented decisions result in a 'set it and forget it' mindset and are the breeding ground for the "but we've always done it that way" limitation.

Therefore, these technical or process-oriented decisions are best suited for static environments when supervision is not as important.

It's also important to remember that the folks that have the technical knowledge are usually operating closest to the process at hand. Even though they also have the best situational awareness, or "ground truth," they may not be the same people initially responsible for making the decision. Therefore, ensuring that the decision-makers, along with those implementing the decision, remain in close communication.

So, while it may be helpful to automate their processes, the decision to revise, innovate or reconfigure that process is best shared with those with the first-hand, technical know-how.

How it helps you: Establishing processes that achieve consist and desired results (like filing certain documents, a certain way, and in a certain place) reduces the time you need to spend managing each task individually.

Hierarchal or Role-Based Decisions

These are the decisions that organizations determine should or should not be made based on where in the hierarchy the decision-maker is.

Examples would be requiring a manager to sign-off on a single expenditure more than $10,000 or permitting only a certain level of employee access the lunch room, server location, parking space, etc.

Administrative decisions tend to fall in line with titles and hierarchy. However, for the dynamic nature of crisis response, decisions made by competent people with the best situational awareness will likely produce the best results.

<u>Some notes about decision-making authority:</u>

Many times, these scripted, technical, and hierarchical decisions get memorialized in a policy manual somewhere. Sometimes for a good reason and sometimes simply because 'that's the way we've always done it.' In either case, the progressive Response Leader should evaluate and seek to improve the quality and applicability of these scripted policy manual decisions. They often become outdated and restrictive.

Occasionally review and scrub any organizational policy that too narrowly defines who has decision-making authority. Any authority for decision-making delegated further down the organization empowers and engages workers lower in the organization and frees up workers higher in the organization. That creates a winning combination.

Stay mindful, however, that while the benefits of delegating decision-making authority are self-evident, some may feel eviscerated if they lose their authority to make a decision. Address these concerns head-on and prepare to explain in greater detail 'why' delegating their authority is beneficial to everyone, including them.

How it helps you: Facilitating role-based decision-making may be appropriate when seeking to institutionalize how and whom should make a particular decision.

Circle of Competence

The Circle of Competence is linked to our decision-making and describes the breadth of knowledge we have on a given topic. Conceived by famed investor Warren Buffett and mainly used for investors to "stay in their lane," the Circle of Competence offers a helpful framework for our leadership decision-making.

The volume of knowledge is important, of course, but good leaders that are surrounded by smart people can usually aggregate quite a bit of knowledge to augment what they know.

More important to understanding our Circle of Competence is our awareness of the point we transition from making decisions based on what we know to decisions based on what we don't know. The line marking that transition defines our Circle of Competence.

Referring to our technical and hierarchical decisions, we may find that those making decisions higher up in the hierarchy do not have the technical knowledge to make an informed decision. In that case, they would be making decisions outside of their Circle of Competence.

Here's how it frequently plays out in disasters:

> Fire Chief Franklin has been 'off the line' and in an office setting for the last several years. He knows that there have been advances in how best to respond to a wide area disaster, but he has never personally received any training on what those advances are or how to apply them.

> Regardless, when a tornado strikes his community, he takes command of the response and makes decisions based on what he believes about disaster response best practices. Unfortunately, he crossed the line from what he knew, regardless how limited his knowledge was, to an area where he had little competence. His leadership suffered of course, but more importantly, the response suffered also because he didn't know when to say "I don't know," and he didn't seek out someone who did have the decision-making competence he needed.

The difference between knowing and understanding is the boundary of your Circle of Competence.

Successful Response Leaders focus their decision-making efforts on what is within their Circle of Competence.

What if they need to decide on a topic outside their Circle of Competence?

They do more homework on the topic, or they delegate the decision to someone whose competence includes the topic at hand.

How it helps you: Knowledge of your limitation about a topic also accompanies the power to find someone to help you whose competencies are on that same topic.

Later we will further our discussion and include the use of "The Red Slice." It will expand our understanding how recognizing the limitations of our knowledge is critical for Response Leaders.

Centralized Decisions

Centralized decisions are decisions made by Response Leaders centrally located in the organization, usually at the top of the organization and emanating from the command post. Because centralized decisions tend to originate from the command post, they also tend to be hierarchal.

By making these centralized decisions, they can be coordinated more easily how they will be carried out at the command level. By communicating these high-level decisions from the top down, it's easier for everyone involved in the event response to understand and follow the same set of instructions.

Example:

1. The event coordinator decided to have the command post, and the Staging Area set up on the north side of the elementary school.
2. Accomplish the following six objectives before we go home.

It's important to note that centralized decision-making is not the same as empowered decision-making or decentralized decision-making, discussed later.

How it helps you: When collecting the best information about the crisis in one place, over-arching decisions based on that information tend to produce better outcomes.

Short versus Long-Term Decisions and Their Consequences

My parents used to tell me when I was about to make an ill-informed choice:

"Don't write a check that your butt can't cash."

When we're young, we tend to decide things without a great deal of forethought. Like when I was 15 years old, and I shaved my legs to be more competitive in a triathlon, not considering the social impact of showing up to school with razor stubble on my legs for weeks afterward.

During a crisis, Response Leaders must show a little more forethought than a 15-year-old boy with shaved legs.

"For every action, there is an equal and opposite reaction." ~ Sir Isaac Newton

---

In the action of decision-making, this is certainly true. And those decisions produce short-term reactions (consequences) or long-term reactions (consequences).

Short-Term Consequences

Decision: Order coffee with cream, forgot you don't like cream.

Consequence: Power through the cup of coffee and drink black coffee next time.

Decision: Don't notify other departments of scheduled planning meeting.
Consequence: Goodwill damaged until the decision-maker makes amends.

Long-Term Consequences

Decision: Get a tattoo of Van Halen on your chest when you're 21-years old.
Consequence: Explain to your kids and grandkids why the ink splotch of David Lee Roth looks so scary.

Decision: Delay telling your community to evacuate due to the rising flood water.
Consequence: Lives lost.

There's another factor to overlay on short and long-term consequences: *The impact.*

The easiest decisions to manage are low impact and short-term, like adding unwanted cream to your coffee.

The other end of the spectrum is the high-impact and long-term, like burning your house down after deciding to leave the candles burning while you're gone to make the place smell good.

Here's an illustration of the long/short-term consequence plus their impact:

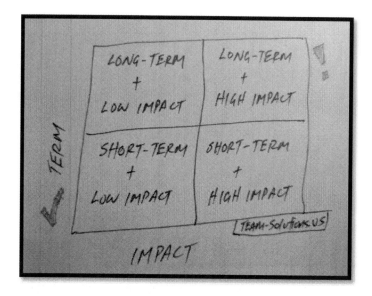

How it helps you: By maintaining awareness of how long you have to live with the consequences of your actions, your decision-making improves.

Empowered Decisions

When centralized and coordinated decisions are passed down from on high, it's up to the Response Leaders in the field to carry them out.

Response Leaders at every level understand that when they delegate instructions and authority, the recipient of those instructions should also be empowered to carry them out.

Example:

The Facilities Unit Leader asks Fred to get 30 chairs from storage to put in the meeting room. Since Fred is expected to accomplish that task, Fred should, therefore, be empowered to take a company truck and to check out a key to the storage area in order to complete the task.

Empowerment is the fuel that moves objectives forward.

Control v. Empowerment

When balancing control versus empowerment, consider this:

- **Controlling** the decision-making process is appropriate when the team member has *low competence* or *low clarity* in the task at hand
- **Empowering** the decision-making process is appropriate – and less control is needed - when the team member exhibits *high competence* and *high clarity* in the task at hand.

Example:

At different times in my response career, I've needed the benefit of a dynamic rope rescue system to move a person in need (me, sometimes!) upward or downward. I've received advanced rope rescue training but am not what one would call a practitioner; I seldom use the skills.

If Little Timmy fell into a well with his pony, I would not be the best choice to be empowered to decide how to build a rope system to rescue them. Even though my clarity of the task may be high, my competence in deciding on the required steps to building a rope system would be low.

In that instance, more control over my decision-making activities would be needed by the team leader.

On the other hand, if another team member possessed oodles of competence and clarity on how to build and use a complex rope system, then the leader could rightly relinquish much more decision-making power.

US military doctrine uses "mission command" to enable centralized command/control with decentralized execution. Subordinate commanders are given mission objectives and then empowered to devise local tactics to achieve them. Military leaders do not tell subordinate commanders how to do it, only what they are expected to do.

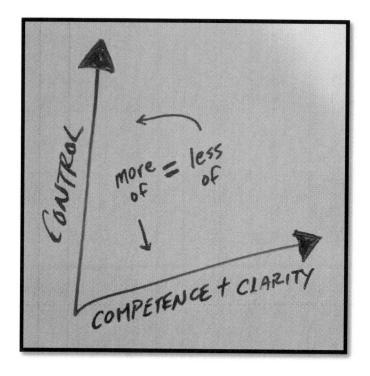

How it helps you: By maintaining awareness of how much competence and clarity your team has, you'll be better informed about how and when to exercise greater control.

Using a Decision Tree

Decision trees are a kind of 'either/or' flowchart that works well when you have time to ponder the different decision-making types and their possible outcomes.

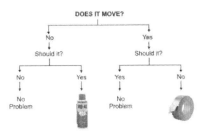

To maximize the benefit of using a decision tree, measure each step against the five primary types of decisions we make:

1. **Delayed** – wait until later
2. **Rapid** – quick and short
3. **Deferred** – pass off to someone else
4. **Strategic** – analyze all of the options
5. **Consequential** – must be ready to justify

Example of a decision tree:

I work out of a home office where I toil away all hours of the day and night when I'm not traveling. Because I'm in a shared space with my family, I also have an open-door policy for my family to come into my office whenever they want for whatever reason they want.

When I am doing brain work, like conceiving an article or course material, that seems to be when my son wants to discuss whether he should attend a birthday party for a classmate instead of attending soccer practice.

My decision tree during these interruptions looks like this:

Delayed decision: *"Not now, Mijo."*

> Pro: The quickest route to return to my task, but the lingering question may impede my focus.

> Con: The progress on my son's day slows considerably.

Rapid decision: *"Yes"* or *"No,"* with little explanation.

Pro: Get back to my task sooner.

Con: May leave my son with uncertainty about our current level of connection.

Deferred decision: *"Go ask your Mother."*

Pro: Acknowledge that there's a decision to be made, just not by me.

Con: Family recognizes my lack of helpfulness.

Strategic decision: Ask *"what does your best judgment tell you?"*

Pro: Empowers my son to use his brain.

Con: May reduce his interest in coming to me when I do need to contribute to his answer.

Consequential decision: *"I need to research the possible outcomes to ensure that your choice is justified."*

Pro: Good awareness promotes good results.

Con: May needlessly complicate or delay a simple decision.

How it helps you: Using a decision tree is less helpful in real time but is worth considering when you're refining your mental mindset.

Emotion versus Logic

Let's be real; a crisis is overflowing with different emotions.

If you've ever argued with someone and said or did something you regret because 'your emotion got the better of you,' you're familiar with this condition.

During a crisis:

- Perhaps our family is impacted while deployed and we're trying to serve the greater good and aren't there to help.
- Perhaps we see or experience the dreadful loss of life, safety, property, and sanity.

The advantages to using an emotional connection to our decisions are notable. Even if all our decisions are devoid of emotion (unlikely), some emotional connection to the task is helpful:

- We're more likely to decide to send help to Little Timmy before deciding to order meals for the team.
- We're more likely to consider the impact on our customer's safety before considering the impact to our shareholder's profits.

In fact, research conducted by neuroscientists at Florida State University indicates that emotions are an important input used in making good decisions. Emotions tend to focus our attention on the options most likely to lead to a positive outcome and rule out the options most likely to lead to a negative outcome.

Typically, however, using logic more than emotion enables a path to clearer decision-making.

The advantages to using a more logical approach to decision-making are also notable.

- We're more likely to 'do the best, for the most.'

    o For example, deciding to help the ten people trapped inside building A is more logical than first helping the one person trapped inside building B.

Having the emotional intelligence to care deeply about the mission and the people impacted by the crisis is an attribute for any world-class Response Leader. Emotional intelligence is addressed more thoroughly in a separate topic.

How it helps you: Emotions are part of what makes you human, but as a Response Leader, also stay vigilant on knowing emotion's role in your decision-making.

Consensus and Probability-Based Decision-Making

In the early 1970's if Little Timmy got lost in the woods, search managers would search using the method I call 'searching by inevitability.' This approach assumes that if searchers cover enough territory, enough times, for long enough, they will eventually find Little Timmy. Searching by inevitability relied on pure luck for Little Timmy to be found early enough in the incident to be still viable.

In the mid-seventies, a gentleman named R.J. Mattson came along and started using a probability consensus method that later became known appropriately as the "Mattson Consensus."

The Mattson Consensus method utilized experts to determine the probable area (or Probability of Area – POA for search folks) where searchers should look for Little Timmy using a simple, mathematical consensus.

1. If ten land areas are identified and segmented for searching, several experts convene to evaluate which area to focus on first.
2. They are allotted 100 percentage points to apply to those ten segments. I.e., Searcher Sam may believe that, based on his experience, Segment 4 has a 50% probability to contain Little Timmy, Segment 6 has a 20% probability and the other 30% probability is spread equally across the remaining eight segments, including the R.O.W., or 'rest of the world.'
3. Each expert weighs in, and the segment with the highest average percentage of probability becomes the consensus winner. Searchers are dispatched, expecting to find Little Timmy there.

Since then, more mathematics-minded folks have improved and in some cases complicated Mattson's method. For the Response Leader desiring to make better decisions, however, a Mattson Consensus still provides simple, useful guidance.

An example of incident decision-making:

The owner of the fictional Hilltop Hotel just learned that its long-serving front desk manager is under arrest on sexual assault charges. The owner assembles her executive staff to decide on a course of action. Their brainstormed options are:

1. Fire the manager immediately, keep the matter quiet, offer no explanation.
2. Fire the manager immediately, notify the staff and guests separately, providing limited details.
3. Notify the staff and guests separately, wait for a confirmation of guilt before deciding on the manager's employment status.
4. Suspend the manager with pay pending the outcome of the case.
5. Allow the manager to continue working, pay for their legal defense.

These options, as well as many other combinations, may all seem viable for the executive team, with different probabilities of a successful outcome for each one.

For example, the option to "suspend the manager" may score an average of a 50% solution for many of the team, while the average consensus for the "fire the manager" option may only score an average of 43%. This result provides the owner a sound basis to decide to suspend the manager with the executive team's support.

When a pool of experts is available, applying a Mattson-type consensus method allows each expert to apply their own experiences to suggest the best course of action.

How it helps you: By reaching a well-constructed consensus, the probability of success increases.

Stress Testing Decisions

Stress testing is done by simulating probable outcomes based on a projected crisis or stressful condition.

Stress testing our ideas, beliefs, and decisions helps us avoid the trap of believing and committing to something that's wrong (or right) simply because we didn't allow our decision to be placed under the bright light of public or colleague scrutiny.

Example:

At dinner many years ago with some friends, I decided – on my own - to eat the whole jar of tabasco peppers that taunted me from the basket of condiments on the table. The very short-term result was some chuckles from my friends. The medium-term result was that I could barely taste food or use the bathroom without pain for nearly a week afterward.

Should I have stress-tested my plan by simulating probable outcomes before following through with it? You decide.

There are, of course, greater consequences for the Response Leader who leans too far ahead with their solo decisions. This dilemma is especially true when there are other capable Response Leaders with whom they can confer.

How it helps you: Stress-testing your decisions before implementing them helps you see deficiencies before being negatively impacted by them.

P.O.S.T. Decisions

Once the key, initial decisions are made, Response Leaders can begin anticipating and formulating the next decisions required in The Response Leadership Sequence™.

On a grand scale, they are:

1. **Priorities**
2. **Objectives**
3. **Strategies**
4. **Tactics**

Each of these is discussed in detail separately. As a primer, let's consider the fate of Bill.

Have you heard this story about "Bill" and his successful project pre-plan? It goes like this:

Bill needs to clean his garage so his wife can park her new car inside before the summer heat arrives.

Bill decides that before the end of Memorial Day weekend he'll donate old items, put away his tools and containerize the camping gear.

Bill determines that he needs to schedule a trip to Goodwill and he needs new storage bins and a bigger toolbox from Home Depot.

Bill acquires what he needs before for the weekend, donates the old stuff, boxes up and stores the camping stuff and reorganizes his tools.

Oh, and when he completes the task, Bill sits back with a cold beverage along with his happy wife. Mission accomplished!

Go, Bill!

A pretty straightforward project that we can all likely relate too, right?

However, when we receive a task to define and execute priorities, objectives, strategies, and tactics, we often freeze up while trying to remember which is which and in which order.

To improve your mission - any mission - remember to plant a P.O.S.T. first:

P.O.S.T. = Priorities + Objectives + Strategies + Tactics

Priorities address the WHY question of your mission. In an emergency response environment, this answer is *"to maximize Life Safety: yours, your team's and your victims ... in that order."*

Objectives address the WHAT questions. Specifically, what future condition indicates the end of the mission? These are the specific, measurable, achievable, relevant and time-bound. You know, S.M.A.R.T.

Strategies address the Big, Conceptual HOW questions. *How will the objectives be met?*

Tactics address the Small, Specific HOW questions. *How will the strategies be executed?*

Let's revisit ol' Bill and his garage project.

Bill needs to clean the garage - Since his wife's happiness is important, that's his priority.

Bill creates specific objectives that will measure his accomplishment. One may be to "donate two bags of old clothes to Goodwill by Saturday at 5 pm".

Bill strategizes the most effective approach to achieve that objective, like "search through each closet for clothes not worn in 6 months".

Bill executes each tactic needed to achieve his objectives, like "sort the clothes into kid clothes and adult clothes, bag them and then drive them to Goodwill."

Each phase has an important role in addressing his priority and each phase in isolation is unlikely to be successful.

- Priorities without specific objectives remain an uninitiated dream.
- Objectives without a strategy do not get accomplished.
- Strategies without tactics are plans without action.
- Tactics without direction can be aimless or even counterproductive busy work.

NOTE: In the inevitable haze and confusion of a complex mission, the Objectives are where we look for clarity. If you only identify one part of your POST, make sure it's the Objectives.

For example: If Bill were to find himself wanting to sit on the couch to watch re-runs of Gunsmoke on TV instead of cleaning the garage, then he simply measures the action of watching TV with the stated Objective of cleaning the garage. If watching TV doesn't support the garage Objective, Bill will have clear evidence that he must re-engage on the garage objective or change his objectives to include watching TV.

He may have a poorly articulated priority, a poor strategy, and poor tactics, but if he has clear Objectives, he'll always have a clear target to shoot.

So the next time you're cleaning the garage, climbing Mount Kilimanjaro or organizing a response to a tornado, remember to plant a POST first.

How it helps you: Using a sensible process to build your decision-making foundation helps when a stressful crisis requires your solid and decisive action.

"Strategy without tactics is the slowest route to victory. Tactics without strategy are the noise before defeat." ~ *Sun Tzu*

Impediments to Good Decision-Making

As far as decision-making goes, we're not as rational as we think, we're not as prepared as we think, and we don't gather as much of the information we think we need.

To improve our decision-making, we must also reduce some common impediments.

Decisions vs. Choices

*"We need to **decide** where to buy a retirement home."*
*"We need to **decide** to order our eggs scrambled or over-easy."*

Both examples are decisions, but only one needs extensive pondering and evaluation before deciding.

By giving the word "decision" the same amount of power in each example, we're more likely to labor over deciding on breakfast needlessly.

During an unplanned event, this needless pondering impedes quick and deliberate decision-making.

Instead, if we look at *decisions* with a high-consequence mindset and *choices*, like which eggs to order, with a low-consequence mindset, our decision-making is less impeded. Such as:

*"I **decided** to ask her to marry me."*
*"I **chose** the right lane instead of the passing lane."*

Or

*"I **decided** to delay sending responders into the field to help the victims until the severe weather subsides."*
*"I **choose** to sleep on the cot near the door."*

Ideas are Not 'Stress-Tested'

As mentioned previously, stress-testing our decisions before making the decision final enables some last-minute course corrections. Stress-testing our decisions, however, also subjects us to ridicule which is why many Response Leaders shy away from openly sharing their thought process in advance.

Nonetheless, Response Leaders with the courage to reveal their thought process to their peers will receive eminently better insight and consult than if they keep the process to themselves.

All Decisions Treated Like Emergencies

"When the only tool you have is a hammer, every problem begins to resemble a nail." ~ Abraham Maslow

---

In decision-making parlance, *'when the only way we know to make a decision is strident and quick, we tend to apply that method to every decision.'*

For a non-emergent decision that addresses a future occurrence - like a hurricane with 96-hours' notice before landfall – emergency decisions are often misplaced.

Unfortunately, and fortunately, many Crisis Response Leaders are accustomed to making strident, commanding decisions in the heat of battle. Once these often-forceful decisions become habituated, they use the same approach when deciding between chicken or fish at the restaurant with their family; even when they would have chosen the flank steak if they just took a moment to think about it.

One way to overcome this tendency and start making measured and informed decisions is to write down the decision trigger and the outcome. When you can see the cause and effect of each choice, you can evaluate the quality of those choices historically and learn to diversify the way you make future decisions.

We have Bias

Bias is an inclination or prejudice for or against someone or something.

- A bias toward being around happy and healthy people is good.
- A bias against including others that don't think like us is not-so-good.

The majority of cognitive biases are intended to simplify our decision-making by saving the mental energy required to consider and incorporate other beliefs. However, simple decisions must also be balanced by any inherent bias that can also reduce the quality of those decisions.

Below are three other common biases that hinder our decision-making. Reduce their impact and increase your positive results.

Complexity Bias

While the simple option is often the best option (Occam's Razor), be mindful of the tendency to add complexity where it may not exist.

- <u>Example:</u> when a computer starts acting wonky, our bias toward complexity leads us to believe that it is a virus, requires professional service, etc. when the simple solution is to turn it off for 30 seconds and then turn it back on.

A Complexity Bias leads us to add more weight to a complex concept with little or no basis.

We see this bias frequently in marketing, where cars, supplements, shampoos, etc. are labeled with complex features to lead the buyer into thinking that the product is superior to the competitor.

Recency Bias

This common phenomenon occurs when the Response Leader only considers the most recent data before making a decision.

- Example: an investor that looks only at a recent decline in stock prices as the reason for selling fails to consider the overall increase in stock prices over the last decade.

Evaluate long-term decisions as far back in history as you do forward in the future to reduce the ill-effects of this bias.

Confirmation Bias

"I think therefore I am." ~ René Descartes

Great bromide for building confidence, for sure. But that mindset also forms the basis of confirmation bias, or tendency to expend effort only on those ideas that conform to one's existing opinion.

- Example: believing that all firefighters arrive on the scene with an existing abundance of operational ICS knowledge can reduce or remove the incentive to provide them additional training or expand the responder pool to include others that also have ICS experience.

If circumstances permit, Response Leaders should seek outside counsel from someone with a different perspective before making a big decision.

Over-Confidence

We can agree that too much of anything is usually not a good thing. Confidence included.

Overconfidence obscures our ability to make good predictions and leads us to overestimate our abilities.

As I describe in my upcoming breakdown of the "Red Slice," we simply *"do not know what we do not know."* And this creates a dangerous environment for decision-making.

Keep your confidence balanced with reality to maximize the results of your decision-making.

Limited Choices

"Paper or Plastic?"

or

"Do you call everyone into the office on a Sunday morning to respond to rumors of a data breach, or do you wait until you have more information before calling everyone?"

Choices that are too narrowly defined lend themselves to deficient decision-making. The reality is that choices are seldom 'just this' or 'just that,' they exist on more of a continuum.

In the example above, the objective is likely to stay ahead of the perilous impact of a data breach. Therefore, calling select members of the team to help confirm the reports is probably a better interim step than calling all of them or none of them.

Widen your initial choices to avoid limiting your potential outcomes.

Buyer's Remorse

Several years back, my television of nearly 17 years finally died. High Definition TV's were new, so I researched them up and down for weeks before finally making a decision which one to purchase.

My selection cost more than any TV in my short but meaningful TV purchasing history. I was sick to my stomach with the belief that I paid too much, researched too little and that a better choice was probably just around the next corner had I bothered to keep looking.

That's buyer's remorse, and it's prone to happen with any decision we feel uncertain about, particularly big decisions.

- Uncertain about sending the crew home to save money when a threat may still exist?
- Uncertain about sharing details of a recent failure with the Team?

Interestingly, studies show that even if we extensively research our topic before making a decision, our level of satisfaction is essentially no different than when we make a speedier, less-informed decision. Our level of buyer's remorse, in other words, is tied more to our confidence in making the decision, not whether we labored over the data first.

This buyer's remorse is evident in the High-Speed Decisions v. Analysis Paralysis example of choosing a meal from a comprehensive menu.

Perhaps that is why the insanely customer-centric folks at Amazon.com practice what's called High-Velocity Decision-Making. They aim to make decisions quickly when they have about 70% of the available information they need.

On the occasion when not if their decision produces less than the desired result, they simply course-correct until they achieve the desired result.

The bottom line is this: waiting for more information takes longer, slows the decision, but seldom improves the result.

Oh, when we eventually upgraded that HD TV to an even newer model, we visited the store, asked a few questions, and walked out with a new TV. We haven't look back, and we're still enjoying that purchase today.

Experiencing Disagreement or Push-Back

In the real world, not every decision we make will be popular. Deciding to host a small and low-key birthday party for our son instead of flying him and his friends to Barcelona so he can watch his favorite soccer team play, the most recent example.

Professionals are adept at dealing with the disappointment of a decision that doesn't go their way. But not everybody is a professional in that regard.

If we're on the delivery end of a decision that's not well-received, we can jeopardize some or all of the goodwill we have built up in that relationship.

If we're on the receiving end of a decision that we don't like, we can lose faith and trust in the person who is 'forcing such an ill-conceived choice on us.'

Autocratic or command and control leadership-types will tend to steamroll over any detractors, but most of us need a better solution.

Since we're speaking about a crisis, a lengthy negotiation for common ground is not advisable. For leadership guidance during a crisis, I've found the words of now-retired General Colin Powell to be particularly useful:

"When we are debating an issue, loyalty means giving me your honest opinion, whether you think I'll like it or not. Disagreement, at this stage, stimulates me. But once a decision has been made, the debate ends. From that point on, loyalty means executing the decision as if it were your own." ~ Colin Powell

---

Still, since not everyone has the power and influence of General Powell, a more diplomatic approach to our detractors is needed.

Regardless what side of the disagreement we're on, the issue is usually more about the lack of support needed to move forward than the fact that there's a disagreement.

Support and agreement are not the same things.

Therefore, throwing our hands up in defeat, agreeing to 'agree to disagree,' and sulking in a corner are not attributes we want in a Response Leader.

Instead, respectfully state the reasons for disagreement – if appropriate to do so – and then offer support to move forward anyway. Providing there's a modicum of trust already, this tactic enables the initiative to move forward with everyone's support, even if it doesn't have everyone's agreement.

For example:

Your team is discussing plans for your upcoming Table Top Exercise (TTX) focused on your organization's severe weather response. Sharon is the coordinator and suggests sharing the exercise injects (decision points) in advance with all of the participants.

You state your disagreement to Sharon and explain why. If properly mentored, you tell her, the participants will gain more from the exercise if they receive the injects during the flow of the exercise, similar to decision-making in the real world. You add that providing the injects in advance is kind of like giving students the answers to their exam, before taking it.

However, instead of remaining in a place of defiance, you add that you will support the plan to move forward providing that your disagreement has been heard and considered.

By separating the role of disagreement and support, we can keep the process moving forward and minimize any damage to our relationships.

Decision fatigue

Columbia University conducted a study opining that the average person in America makes 70 conscious decisions every day.

Now imagine doing 70 pushups over the course of an entire a day. Early in the day, they are easier. After a break, they are easier. After a sequence of too many pushups at one time or late in the day they are more difficult. Your pushup form erodes and your muscles fatigue.

The same is true with decision-making. It's a muscle that is susceptible to fatigue and eventual collapse.

Watch or read the news, and you'll see that most of the bad decisions that people make featured in the news occur late in the day. Decision fatigue is real.

As a Response Leader, make as many important decisions while you are rested and defer or delegate decisions when you are mentally fatigued.

Decision-Making Summary

"In any moment of decision, the best thing you can do is the right thing, the next best thing is the wrong thing, and the worst thing you can do is nothing." ~ Theodore Roosevelt

---

A good decision doesn't guarantee your success any more than a bad decision seals your fate.

Therefore, the worst decision is the decision never made.

All of the decision-making models presented are a heuristic or "rule of thumb" to reference quickly. They are not expected to be optimal for every instance but rather practical for any instance.

Remember, too; the intent behind good decision-making is to solve a problem. Deciding that you prefer chocolate ice-cream over vanilla ice-cream offers no value if you're not hungry for dessert.

Once you know the problem that needs addressing with your decision, consider your options, rely on your training, and then confidently make a choice!

Some other helpful reminders about competent decision-making:

- Delegate decision-making authority lower in your organization
- Stay within your area of competence when making a decision
- Ask others that have faced similar decisions for guidance and insight
- Widen your options to reduce defining your choices too narrowly
- Reduce your biases by expanding your pool of trusted advisors
- Pace yourself and stay alert to the ill-effects of decisions made while fatigued
- Recognize and control excess emotion playing a part in your decisions
- Avoid overconfidence by accepting our natural human deficiencies; there's no 100% solution

- Stay patient; not all decisions are emergencies

Some may dispute my statement that there's no such thing as a 100% solution so let me address that.

The Myth of 100%

My Response Leadership background has deep roots in search and rescue. I've responded to hundreds of local, regional and national level events to search for all sorts of people, in all sorts of conditions, in all sorts of places.

Sometimes we found whom we were looking for and sometimes we didn't. When we didn't, it was because the missing person was actually in the R.O.W. or "rest of the world" other than where we were looking. Like looking for the dementia patient in the woods while he was 1000 miles away at a casino. (Yes, that happened.)

When you find the person that you're looking for, it's common to say that you've achieved 100% of the objective. While that's certainly defensible, that mindset doesn't help much after a disaster when you don't know – nor will you ever know – how many people are actually lost and missing.

That's why the best searchers are the ones that focus on effectively searching more than effectively finding.

You see, they know that accomplishing a 100% solution in the search for an unknown number of people doesn't exist, so they're not going to hurt themselves trying.

In the broader scope of Response Leadership, the same lesson applies.

I've seen people hurt themselves professionally trying to plan for and achieve a mythical, perfect solution. All that effort comes at the expense of all of the good they could be doing pursuing a more realistic goal.

In fact, even when there is only one known person missing, many search managers will stop looking for you when they're only 80% confident that you're not there.

As previously mentioned, the leadership at Amazon.com have adopted a 70% solution to their decision-making strategy.

1. If they have 70% of a solution, they make a decision.
2. If that decision needs refinement after the introduction of new information, they quickly 'course-correct' and update their decision.

In event response, being the 'best (100%)' is not achievable nor sustainable. However, 'good' Response Leaders will always be in demand.

"The best is the enemy of the good." ~ François-Marie Arouet (aka "Voltaire")

Unifying the Plan and the Wheel of Engagement ™

Your D.U.F.F.E.L. B.A.G.:

1. Developing
2. **_Unifying_**
3. Forecasting
4. Funding
5. Equipping
6. Learning
7. Boosting
8. Assessing
9. Getting Ready to Act

"My responsibility is to get my twenty-five guys playing for the name on the front of their uniform and not the name on the back." ~ Tommy Lasorda

---

After developing the initial framework, it may be appropriate to start building a team of other Response Leaders to help you unify the plan.

The simplest choices often end up as one of the biggest problems so careful consideration must be given before adding to your team. Here's an example of what I mean:

The city manager directs the police department to develop a special event plan, with contingencies, for this fall's parade. The police assemble their planning team consisting of:

1. Two senior police officers
2. Two junior police officers
3. "Jerry" from the Streets Department

They cobble together a plan based on their knowledge, experience, and perspective. The city manager who may not know any better approves of the plan.

Fast forward to the fall parade.

- One of the parade floats catches fire and crashes into the crowd of spectators and then knocks down a power pole.
- Spectators – some injured - flee in all directions and snarl the traffic flow in the immediate area.
- The local hospital is overrun with people self-reporting their injuries.
- Some parents cannot find their children in the melee and clog the 911 system crying for help.
- Social media is reporting that it was a terrorist attack.
- Local businesses have to shut down because of the growing unrest.

The result of the city manager's investigation showed the following entities had valuable contributions that were available for the event plan but were not included (mental model: "Selection Bias").

1. the fire department
2. the hospital
3. the ambulance service
4. the citizen volunteers
5. the business community
6. the emergency managers, etc.

The police department is embarrassed but incredulous about including others in 'their' plan. The jilted organizations lose trust and respect for the police department and eventually each other as each of them search for relevancy and power.

When the time to plan for the next parade rolls around, the divisions between the groups has grown even deeper. Even under direct orders to work together, the group is neither inclusive or productive.

The parade ends up being a disjointed display of ego, political posturing, and ineptitude.

In 20+ years I've seen a similar dynamic play out in the public sector and the private sector. And I could have just as easily made the fire department, the emergency manager, the citizen volunteer group or the business continuity manager the 'star' of the show.

The core issue with these decision-makers tends to fall in one of below categories:

1. They are **unwilling**
2. They are **unable**
3. They are **unaware**

In analyzing these ridiculous *'silos of excellence,'* the names and faces may change, but the results stay the same.

The solution, however, tends to fall into just one category: **better leadership**.

As discussed, successful Response Leaders always *"begin with the end in mind."*

Believe it or not, leaders can and do benefit from the support and cooperation of diverse or competing Response Leaders. They do so by building them into their planning process sooner than later.

Even when challenging, building the right coalition at the beginning enables future efforts to be more robust, more informed and more resilient.

Recruitment

Where do Response Leaders come from?

Ideally, they're built from the ground up.

Here are some fundamental strengths that team-building thought leaders like Warren Buffet, Patrick Lencioni, Dave Ramsey, and Jeff Bezos look for:

- Smart
- Hungry
- Integrity
- Team player
- Winners attitude
- Reasonable

- Energetic
- Considerate
- Humble
- Honest
- Resourceful

If you can find someone that exhibits these strengths, they can be trained to do almost anything.

Therefore, Response Leaders are potentially everywhere.

And I'm actually using the strictest definition of a Response Leader too, as discussed in this program:

- Knows and Understands the significance of WHY and WHAT
- Knows and Understands SMART Objectives
- Knows and Understands The Response Leadership Sequence™
- Knows and Understands how to engage with other Response Leaders
- Knows and Understands the purpose and the general mechanics of functional leadership
- Knows and Understands the importance of honesty
- Knows and Understands how to communicate
- Knows and Understands the key aspects of the Response Leaders Mindset
- Knows and Understands the basics of contingency planning
- Knows and Understands how to develop a Readiness to Act

Notice that nothing on the above hit-list of ideal recruits says anything about subject matter expertise, or an I-Love-Me Wall full of certificates, etc.

Whether they currently serve in an IT department, on a volunteer fire department, as a dog groomer or anything in between, they can immediately add value to our event with the above knowledge.

Once you identify these pools of knowledgeable souls, more pre-work is needed. As discussed separately, there may be an agency or departmental agreements or other 'kitchen passes' that are necessary to allow the newly identified recruits to be released to come over and serve.

Above and beyond that though is the need actually to build some version of a relationship first. That relationship needs to be a little more advanced than what two dogs do when they meet for the first time, but not by much.

Crisis Response is ultimately a people business, and when one person needs the services of another, a relationship of some type is necessary, first.

In person preferably but by phone, Skype or email if not. We would want to get a sense of whom we are going to battle with, and they deserve the same crack at it as we do.

If the event is already triggered when this relationship building happens, that meeting may also be an outstanding time to share the event's initial objectives!

1. Identify the recruits
2. Facilitate the service
3. Build the relationship
4. Share the Mission

When the pools of recruits do not have a background in Response Leadership, then the resource management strategies discussed separately may help. By knowing what skills are needed, the recruitment process can be refined to only look and recruit where there are ideal, qualified candidates.

Unfortunately, just having a room full of qualified candidates doesn't mean they are brimming with the purpose and passion needed to help the plan succeed.

They must be engaged.

Engagement

"Awareness without engagement is like chewing without swallowing. Tasty, but not very satisfying." ~ *Mike Rowe*

When folks used to say that they wanted "engagement," it meant they wanted an agreement to get married.

Now, engagement is bandied around in organizations as a minimum standard of commitment and emotional involvement for every employee to be measured against.

If they are not deemed engaged enough, then there are focus groups convened, consultants called and team picnics mandated.

However, who among us has ever questioned the validity of the claim that everyone must be engaged at all times, regardless?

The reality is that many, many functions work just fine when implemented by people that are not 'emotionally involved.'

- Does the 16-year-old need to be emotionally committed to delivering a pizza or serving french fries? *No.*
- Does the accountant need to be emotionally committed to balancing the books? *No.*
- Does the sales team need to be emotionally committed to selling widgets to set sales records? *No.*
- Does the janitor need to be emotionally committed to emptying the trash into the dumpster? *No.*

Would it help if those people were committed emotionally to their task? *Perhaps.*

Pendulum Effect

"The pendulum of the mind alternates between sense and nonsense, not between right and wrong." ~ Carl Jung

---

I see this race to make everyone engaged as another product of the pendulum effect. [Mental model: "Regression to the Mean."]

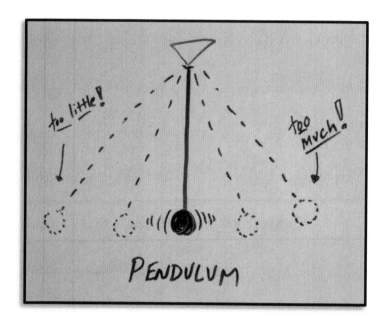

The problem that many people wanted to solve was the lack of emotional commitment some workers had to their jobs.

Bosses concluded that it must be the worker's failure, so the burden to be more engaged was placed on them.

After all, the bosses became bosses because they're engaged so it couldn't be them, right?

That condition pinned the pendulum to one side.

Enter the 'engagement revolution' where employee engagement became the cause célèbre ... and the pendulum immediately swung and became pinned to the opposite side.

The reality is that a proportional amount of engagement is necessary. When fostered genuinely, engagement can ignite tremendous growth and success.

So, on the topic of growth and success, I agree that engagement is critical.

Regarding the examples above, an attitude of growth and success are not required to deliver a pizza, etc. so engagement is merely a nice byproduct when it exists.

For Response Leaders, I could also argue that few things should be more important than engagement; feeling it and promoting it.

However, when engagement doesn't exist, there tend to be two (2), related deficiencies. The lack of:

Passion: *strong emotion*
Purpose: *"why" we do something*

"If you want to build a ship, don't herd people together to collect wood and don't assign them tasks and work, but rather teach them to long for the endless immensity of the sea." ~ Antoine de Saint-Exupéry

---

The traditional view is that when employees don't have passion and purpose, the lack of resolve must be an employee deficiency, not an employer deficiency.

Such is the fate of Millennials (age 18-34). Like the generations before them that also had to endure labels of all sorts, the much-maligned Millennials are the scapegoat for the lack of engagement in many organizations.

It's an argument for the ages because there are no shortcuts to building and maintaining authentic engagement.

There's also not a straight line or cause-and-effect relationship between purpose and passion.

As you'll see, passion and purpose are merely spokes on a wheel.

The TEAM Solutions Wheel of Engagement™

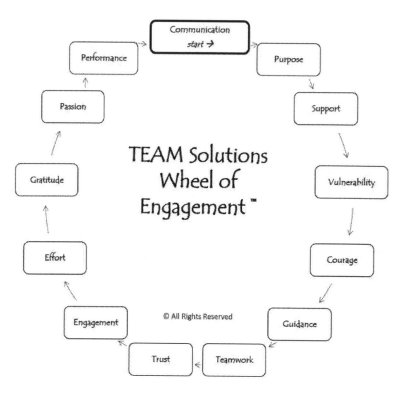

For the Wheel of Engagement ™ to spin and advance down the road, the following spokes are needed:

1. **Communication**
2. **Purpose**
3. **Support**
4. **Vulnerability**
5. **Courage**
6. **Guidance**
7. **Teamwork**
8. **Trust**
9. **Engagement**
10. **Effort**
11. **Gratitude**

12. **Passion**
13. **Performance**

Let's look at Raul's situation as an example.

Leader to Raul: "Hi Raul and welcome to the team.

Our purpose here is to build, sell and deliver widgets.

As the foreman, I aim to provide clear instructions on what our objectives are, to support you in your role here and to remove any obstacles that may be keeping you from being successful. [COMMUNICATION]

Your purpose will be to help add the doo-hicky to the thinga-ma-bob on each widget.

Your contribution will make a huge difference in the success of the team. A success that we will all enjoy together. Do you support that purpose?" [PURPOSE]

"We'll train you how to do that and support you along the way until we're all comfortable with you working with the widgets by yourself. At any time, if you feel unsupported and have a question or unmet need, Monique will be there to mentor you. Okay?" [SUPPORT]

Later...

Raul to Monique: "I've started to fall behind in my production and have had an increase in defective assemblies. I'm also concerned that other team members are starting to think that I don't fit in here as a result of my performance." [VULNERABILITY]

Monique to Raul: "I understand your concern. I've felt that way before too and agree that it's a crummy feeling and an undesirable place to be. What do you think would make a positive difference for you?

Raul: "If I could do my job starting an hour earlier so I can leave an hour earlier. My kid is going through a rough time, and I want to be able to pick her up from school. Worrying about her has impacted my job here." [COURAGE]

Monique to Raul: "Thank you for having the courage to speak up. We don't succeed unless we all succeed so yes, we'll shift your hours. I'll also step in so I can help you get caught up and to make sure you're still comfortable with the precise steps needed to assemble your part of the widget. Lastly, we have our regular scheduled team event coming up which should flush out and address any cohesion issues on the team. Someone will always be here anytime you have a concern or vulnerability so thanks again for speaking up." [GUIDANCE]

Later...

Raul to other team members at team event: "Thanks for showing me the cool tip to make my job easier and for helping out when I got a little behind. It was fun learning a little about your job here too." [TEAMWORK]

"Lastly, thanks for trusting that my setback was only short term and that I do fit in here." [TRUST]

"It does take a team to fulfill our purpose! I look forward to continuing to help this team grow and become even more successful." [ENGAGEMENT]

Later...

Monique to Raul: "Raul, your 1st quarter production numbers are on track to set a new team record. The effort you put into doing exemplary work is noticeable." [EFFORT]

"Your teamwork and willingness to learn are inspirational to all of us. Thanks for your hard work!" [GRATITUDE]

Later...

Raul to Family: "I love my job! It has given me an opportunity to do something valuable, to be in control of the outcome and to strive for a common purpose. My teammates are respectful and supportive, and my mentor is inspiring. I look forward to going to work each day and being a part of that team for a long time!" [PASSION]

Later...

Monique to the Team: "The team's effort set new production records, and everyone will enjoy a share of the subsequent profits. Raul, your extra individual effort with learning the new doo-hickey assembly protocol earned you a free weekend pass to the theme park for your whole family. Great job everyone." [PERFORMANCE]

The leader of the Team: We have grown our market share in making widgets, and we see an opportunity to expand our product line into whatcha-ma-callits. We will face some challenges, but I'm confident that by working together we can overcome them." [COMMUNICATION]

"Our purpose will be to maintain our growth with the widget business and to grow our whatcha-ma-callits business to 20% of our gross revenues by year's end.

That will mean hiring more people into our team. Raul, will you mentor some of our new team members, please? Can everyone support that purpose?" [PURPOSE]

And with that, the Wheel of Engagement™ continues to roll.

I know my example reads like a soap opera, but I intended to illustrate the building blocks of sustainable high performance using a notional example. Did it make you want to build widgets with Raul and Monique?

It's important to note again that many, many missions and projects are accomplished every day without everyone engaged. While the benefits should be self-evident, it is not a do or die proposition.

Now that we've provided the blueprint for organically growing authentic purpose and passion let's look at some specific challenges.

Volunteer Engagement

"Those who can ... do. Those who can do more, volunteer." ~
Anonymous

The unpaid service of selfless volunteers is the lifeblood of many organizations and events.

- Service & Response organizations
- Community parades and festivals
- Holiday special events
- Sports tournaments
- Missing person events
- Weather events
- Community preparedness drills, etc.

They all rely heavily on the force multiplication that trained and reliable volunteers can provide.

Having been on all sides of these scenarios (as a volunteer, event manager, responder, etc.) I can say without hesitation that many of these events would not even exist without access to these selfless and unpaid professionals.

With so many activities that increasingly rely on the service of volunteers, those volunteers that are available can afford to be selective.

However, if their time and service are not valued, they won't be back. Or if they're a member of a volunteer organization, they will disengage.

Volunteer Responders

Above and beyond typical volunteer participation is advanced volunteering, serving with a volunteer organization that responds to a disaster or other crisis-filled environment while everyone else is leaving.

Examples of these organizations may include:

CERT - Community Emergency Response Teams
CAP - Civil Air Patrol
SAR - Volunteer Search & Rescue
ARES/RACES - Amateur Radio Emergency Service/Radio Amateur Civil Emergency Service
ARC - American Red Cross
MRC - Medical Reserve Corps

There are many more credible organizations that rely on unpaid professionals to perform their essential service too.

Volunteer Search & Rescue is how I got my start in Response Leadership, and the role (and subsequent fate) of the volunteer responder has always been near to my heart.

Here is a sample of the feedback I hear from volunteer response organizations I've worked with:

"Team doesn't want to train, only deploy."
"Team only deploys 2x per year ... how do I keep them engaged?"
"How do I manage and motivate our volunteers?"
"How do we attract and keep volunteers?"
"How do we keep them involved even when we're not called out?"

Let's first address some reasons why this condition may exist and then discuss some solutions.

One of the default approaches that almost always fails is to apply pragmatic business logic to the volunteer ranks.

I'm not talking about managing a volunteer organization like a business - which has its benefits - I'm referring to how volunteers get recruited and managed.

Examples of Business logic:

- You must serve X days for Y hours to maintain your membership
- You must serve and support even if we never get called out/deployed
- If you don't take this as seriously as we do, you will not have a future here
- I will withhold X benefit from you until you comply with Y
- Your lack of commitment will keep you from enjoying X opportunity

And finally,

- The Team says/does *"This isn't working out, please turn your stuff in"* and
- The volunteer says/does *"This isn't working out, I'm not going to participate anymore."*

As I've often said: *"we can only do what we're trained to do."* And that applies to every angle here too.

As volunteer Response Leaders, we may have a background in the private sector but have little experience managing volunteers.

- In private sector business and simple terms, people show up to work in exchange for an honest wage.
- As long as there is motivation to get paid and as long as we're holding the purse strings, we can maintain a steady influence over the employee.

However, applying this work-for-reward model to a volunteer who's not there for a living wage leaves many, many Response Leaders unarmed when trying to motivate their 'employee' (volunteer).

Similarly, volunteer Response Leaders who want to serve in a volunteer organization may have an entirely different experience than how this new volunteer organization operates.

In either case, volunteer expectations do not get met, trust does not get built, and the chances for a successful relationship diminish.

While every situation may require a slightly different solution, there are some common solutions to these common, volunteer management challenges.

Attracting Volunteers:

Identify the motivation why someone would volunteer in the first place.

Some volunteers are looking for resume-building community service hours. They may be interested in your mission, but probably not as much they're interested in you signing off that they spend an hour per week with your group. They can still add value to your organization – a rare few may even become long-serving members – but if your recruitment only focuses on this type of volunteer, you'll be chasing your tail trying to retain them because the odds are not in your favor.

Instead, find where the ground is fertile for growing purpose and passion.

Example:

In volunteer search & rescue for teams that utilize search dogs, finding people interested in volunteering is pretty easy. There are lots of dog enthusiasts attracted to the idea of putting a vest on their dog and doing hero stuff that brings attention to themselves and their pup. They will self-identify as being "passionate about dogs."

The faster you show this person a dead body and the reality of a grueling and under-appreciated training regimen that's far from heroic, the sooner you'll know if they also feel the purpose.

Remember, for any measure of lasting engagement; purpose comes long before passion so always start there.

During recruitment, ensure that your messaging focuses on the purpose of your organization and how the recruit can contribute to that purpose.

Example #1:

A group I've worked with used the lure of new equipment and attractive uniforms to recruit new members. The list of new member applicants was full, which led to scarcity, which led to more people wanting to join. The bosses were pleased with the attention and used their applicant list as evidence of their successful team building efforts. Because of the lack of purpose infused into the onboarding process, member retention was abysmal and the recurring cost to constantly train replacement members soared.

Example #2:

A different group ran Facebook advertisements that targeted users who aligned with the group's purpose. They also passed out flyers at stores frequented by the same, target market. Their advertisements, their flyers, and their 'pitch' focused on the group's purpose and announced their interest in working with people who connected to that purpose.

Thoughtful and grassroots growth helps recruit and keep members aligned with your purpose first, then enables growing the relationship using the TEAM Solutions Wheel of Engagement™.

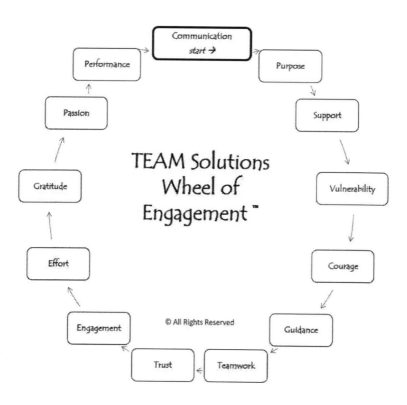

Keeping Volunteers:

Once a volunteer is in the 'system' are they treated like a hunk of meat ... or as an internal customer?

Do we know how much they, or we for that matter, invest of time and money into their volunteer commitment?

The Underreported Costs of Volunteering [Case Study]

The brochure says that volunteering is fun, important, and appreciated.

However, seldom discussed is the significant amount of time and money costs associated with volunteering.

Using search & rescue as an example, let's peel back some of those costs and the impact they have on recruiting and retaining volunteers:

[Case Study] The Costs of Volunteering

"Pat" manages an all-volunteer, Search & Rescue team. The team relies on members that are spread out across four counties. As a new member, "Sam" must meet minimum requirements for 1) training 2) attendance and 3) performance before he can respond to a real search.

That process required before Sam can be deemed 'operational' can take up to a year or more is one of several reasons that many new members like him quit. This delay and subsequent high dropout rate pose a real challenge for Pat and the team. Not having enough qualified members to deploy on real searches can result in serious consequences for the mission to find the lost or missing person.

Many new members like Sam also come from the private sector, where the expectation to be productive is common. They expect that the training is:

- Well organized

THE RESPONSE LEADERSHIP SEQUENCE™

- Time efficient
- Cost-effective
- Valuable for their personal development

Besides the extensive delay in training, frequent dropouts are the result of these failed expectations:

- Too many hours spent driving to and from training, meetings, and seminars
- Too many hours spent attending training, meetings, and seminars
- Too much money spent going to training, conferences, seminars, buying books, etc.

The mission may be better off without people like that, but the fact remains that quality SAR responders are hard to find, train, and keep. Identifying why some decide to leave helps fuel a solution.

Let's expand some detail on Sam's journey:

Like most teams, Sam's team trains once per week and schedules a business meeting each month that often includes a training element. Sam's team also hosts or attends pricey seminars, external training classes, certification courses, buys books, pays for testing fees, etc.

In Sam's case, he also is training a dog for search & rescue. The optional weekly training he attends to work with the team's experienced handlers and the related education is yet another commitment of time and expense.

Not including equipment costs, Sam's annual costs associated with earning an operational status can be gigantic. Remember too, that other volunteer members are also contributing their time to help Sam receive the training he requires.

And that doesn't include the yearly 'maintenance' costs to keep Sam trained and his knowledge refreshed.

So, what's all of that time worth? The non-profit trade group Independent Sector tracks and publishes this data every year:

"The value of a volunteer hour is $24.14, and the value of a volunteer mile is .14 cents." ~ Independent Sector (2016)

Using those figures, here's a conservative breakdown of Sam's volunteer time and expense to participate in his SAR team on a monthly basis:

Activity per MONTH:

- Time spent driving to and from training = 8 hours ($193.12)
- Time spent attending training & meetings = 20 hours ($482.80)
- Time spent attending misc. training, seminars, etc. = 8 hours ($193.12)
- Fees, mileage costs, etc. = $150.00
- Time spent at optional K9 Training = 20 hours ($482.80)
- Time spent by Team member support = 20 hours ($482.80)

That's a minimum of **76 hours** spent volunteering per month valued at **$1834.64**. *Per month.*

In just Sam's first year - before he even goes on his first search - he spends nearly **1000 hours** of time worth over **$22,000**. And he has a 50/50 chance he'll quit before he even gets that far.

These are very conservative estimates, too. In my first year in SAR, I spent nearly TWICE as much time training than the above example.

Sam and other new members like him may spend more or less time on their SAR training compared to the data above. However, any way you slice it, the costs to train a new member are enormous and vastly under-recognized.

If these teams were businesses, they'd be broke and still short of employees.

So, it's easy to see why the burden of time and money breaks the will of many eager SAR prospects, doesn't it?

That huge burden of time and expense is why I offer a wide range of foundational training options for volunteers at TEAM-Solutions.US.

Super-volunteers

Most volunteer organizations are run by what I call super-volunteers.

These super-volunteers have been around the longest, know the most about the organization and summarily elevate to a position of authority. That by itself does not make them a leader.

It's common for these super-volunteers to measure all other volunteers by what they've done, not by what the new volunteer has done or is capable of doing.

Like the challenge with Gen-x-ers and Millennials, this chasm tends only to grow wider. In a moment, I offer some solutions.

Board of Directors

Another area where super-volunteers aren't-so-super occurs after they achieve a certain status within the organization, say, a position on the board of directors.

As a quick aside, the responsibility of the board of directors for a non-profit entity is to *"Give Money, Get Money or Get Off the Board."*

The non-profits that elevate their super-volunteers to the board level sets them up for failure (they seldom have fund-raising experience) and creates lots of other unintended consequences.

Every volunteer has a threshold of time, money, effort that they're willing to invest in a volunteer activity. Even though they may not freely admit it, that includes super-volunteers too.

For some board of director's involvement, every hour spent is really like spending two. It can be that taxing. Since they're super-volunteers, they may also be uncomfortable showing their vulnerability to having invested more energy than they should have.

One way you know their grasp has exceeded their reach is when they stop being a volunteer and start being an overlord.

Another reason on the opposite end of the spectrum why they may disengage from being a volunteer is because they're intoxicated by their status as a super-volunteer.

Coincidentally, that attitude results in the same outward behavior: Overlord instead of a volunteer.

They may feel as if they've paid their dues and that the not-so-super volunteers need to step up and 'do the grunt work.'

While some of that may be righteous at some level, it conflicts with the need to have clear expectations, and relationships suffer as a result.

In other words, the new volunteer is more likely treated like a hunk of meat to be tenderized than as an internal customer that needs cultivating.

Internal Customers

There's no question that many super-volunteers are who sustain many volunteer organizations. They freely give their time and energy and have high expectations for others to do the same.

When the new volunteer (or new internal customer') isn't able or willing to perform at the same level, super-volunteers tend to emotionally abandon the new volunteer and seek out people that are more like them.

Note that the most sought-after organizations to work for all have something in common: workers of all ages feel supported at work.

Investing in the new volunteer (or re-engaging with the recently disengaged volunteer!) as successful businesses do with customers can help keep volunteer participation from going flat.

Because when the Wheel of Engagement™ goes flat, people disengage and leave.

Work Expectations

If there were a history book full of case studies from failed relationships, I surmise that the number one cause would be the disparity in expectations.

> Woman expects the beach
> +
> man expects the big city
> +
> years of arguments about having separate expectations
> =
> *Eventually failed relationship*

You get the idea.

The same is true in the volunteer arena.

> New volunteer expects _____ (lots of activity/deployments, respectful leaders, easy work, etc.)
> +
> Reality (few deployments, disrespectful leaders, hard work, etc.)
> +
> Growing discontent that "this isn't worth the time and effort for so little in return."
> =
> *Eventually failed relationship*

Based on my experience working with disaster response volunteers, this simple example plays out more often than people might think.

Volunteer Engagement [Case Study]:

Here's another look at the volunteer experience from an engagement standpoint instead of just a financial standpoint.

- The volunteer response team has 100 members.
- Meetings are held one time per month on a weeknight for 2 hours (24 hours per year).

- All day training is held one time per month for 6 hours (72 hours per year).
- Each member has to meet a 50 hour per year minimum training and meeting requirement before they're eligible for being called out for a response. Very few meet that annually.
- On average, they get called out four times per year at different times of the day and night.

Super-volunteers run the meetings each month. The agenda covers things like minutes from the last meeting, financial accounting and calendar updates. Meetings sometimes devolve into a session about previous events, which leads to grousing about the lack of call outs, the lack of attendance, the lack of community support or the lack of leadership vision. After 2 hours, people are more than ready to leave. The super-volunteer clique goes out for coffee to discuss the lack of team engagement (aka "why can't they be like us") and the rest of the team send texts to each other about how the team is turning into a big waste of time.

The training session each month involves a similar cast of characters, starting with the instructor aka super-volunteer who knows the material but who is not experienced enough as an adult educator to bring the material to life and make it valuable for the attendees. The lack of engagement riles the super-volunteer who thinks that everyone should be able to perform the task after he told them how to do it. After the training, grousing intensifies, and the texts start flying again. This time people that did not attend the training are included in the texts about how wasteful of a day it was to be talked down to for not knowing something. The others tell themselves that they are glad they didn't go.

When the bells go off, and the volunteer team is asked to respond, everybody shows up in force. (We all want to do what we're trained to do!!)

Since there are no perfect responses, when performance issues inevitably come up, the team's managers immediately point a collective finger at the people that did not attend recent training or meeting or that are merely hovering around the minimum attendance figures.

The agency that requested the volunteer team to show up has started to lose faith in the team and began to avoid using them except during rare events.

Since the volunteer team has promised to bring a full team, every available body is needed to 'fly the flag' during those limited responses. Exceptions start being made to include the people whose attendance numbers have slipped below the minimum, especially for the super-volunteers who have 'earned the right' to skip training and only attend deployments.

Resentment grows.

The grousing and texts intensify and disengagement rules the day.

Perhaps by spelling it out step by step the cause(s) are a little more evident? I've worked with volunteer groups across the country, and sadly, even by changing some of the details, I've found that core scenario repeats itself over and over and over.

In fact, from a recent customer survey asking volunteer responders what their number one challenge was volunteer engagement (recruitment, retention, and management) was the most common answer, by far.

NOTE: This dynamic of volunteer vs. host organization expectation applies to virtually every environment where volunteer support is needed.

I created the Wheel of Engagement™ to remedy this condition.

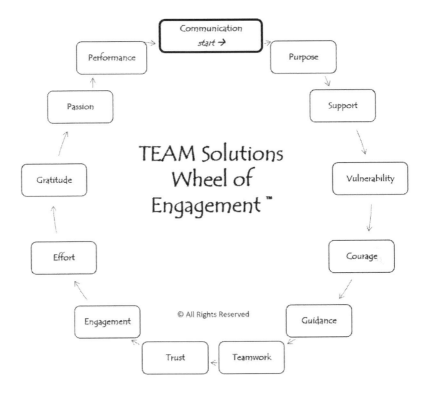

Engagement Solutions

In my previous tale of the growing dysfunction inside the volunteer response team were clues to a solution.

Let's break them down here:

Minimum training requirements

- A baseline amount of training before being deployable is an excellent idea. Putting it on an erratic schedule may not be.
- If a volunteer is on board with the purpose and the other spokes in the Wheel of Engagement™ get addressed, then focus on the training proficiency, not the amount of time spent metric. When the training

connects them to the purpose, they are on the way to sustained passion.

- When focusing on training proficiency, do it right or don't do it at all. Bad training is still training, and bad habits are tough to break.

<u>Minimum meeting requirements</u>

- In today's digital environment, administrative details, meeting minutes, etc. are available for sending electronically. Who wants to give up dinner at home with their family to get a historical account of what happened last month?
- Respect their time, and they will respect you.
- Is a monthly meeting in the same Rec Center meeting room addressing a recognized need?
- Or is it done that way because "we always do it that way?"
- Could the team's business be handled for 10 minutes in the lobby of the local mini-golf course and then the rest of the team "meeting" takes place on the course?
- Or perhaps a field trip for a tour of the local police or fire station?

<u>Low turnout</u>

- Volunteers don't usually start out their volunteer activity by not participating. If they do, that behavior should have been detected and culled in the interview process.
- Low turnout for team events is either:
  - Simple and Explainable: they don't have a babysitter, they're out of town, they're at a family event, etc.
  - Complex and Explainable: their behavior is the accumulation of any or all of the root-causes expressed previously.
  - You fix the root-cause; they fix their low turnout.
- Make the team events valuable. Find out what the membership needs to participate more by asking authentically and not behind the excuse of "but, we've always done it that way."
- Focus on quality, not quantity. Having big member numbers may look good on a grant application, but they grow resentment by active members over time. Give everyone an opportunity to serve within their comfort zone (field workers, administrative workers, advisory board, an auxiliary unit, etc.) or cut them loose and save everybody some time.

Low utilization of team services

- Yes, this is a real buzz-kill. No response volunteer wants to train for 100 hours per month and not get a chance to use their skills during an actual event.
- Being requested by local emergency management agencies (police, fire, etc.) is about trust and awareness.
- Unfortunately, most teams desperate for utilization try to address it by conducting an awareness campaign.

Example:

I served on a volunteer SAR team based in a large metro area (over 7 million people).

We performed search management, K9 search, physical search and light rescue in support of locating lost and missing people due to homicides, suicides, Alzheimer's/dementia walk-aways, child abductions, light disasters, etc.

The majority of our calls came from law enforcement, who were primarily responsible for missing person events.

As more volunteer teams sprung up, there was a concern that our calls for service would go down due to the 'competing services' and the number of agencies that might not know about us.

My team's leadership at the time decided to conduct an awareness campaign to bring our calls for service back up. Their plan involved participating in every parade, carnival, dog-wash, school presentation, etc. where they could include the team.

The result was that the number of service requests went down anyway. Why?

Because the law enforcement agencies that called on us relied on a high level of professional discretion when working on sensitive cases like abductions, murders, etc.

Seeing our team on TV marching in a dog parade did not fill them with confidence that we had their best interests in mind.

They were aware of us now, but not for anything that mattered to them.

We had simply started to lose their trust.

How it changed:

At that time, I handled a certified cadaver (human remains) dog and my tasks consisted of managing most of the human remains related requests.

For a cadaver dog's findings to be used as evidence in a criminal case, the legal standard is: "trained, certified and reliable."

I, therefore, kept extensive records of our training and our searches and made them freely available to any agency.

I also created a fact sheet that illustrated where a cadaver dog can be useful (known starting point, large wooded areas, debris piles, water, etc.) and where their contribution would be less useful (landfill searches, buried deep underground, when the bad guy is still at large, etc.).

I would visit agency representatives that previous used us and would offer a demonstration and to work any cold (unsolved) cases they had.

They didn't seem to care about the demonstration but were very interested in helping to resolve their cold cases where all or part of a body still needed recovering.

I assembled a team to go work on these cold cases and kept the agency updated as often as they could stand it.

We were not always successful, but many times we were.

After submitting a report of our work, I asked for an official letter of thanks and a recommendation, which they were happy to provide.

I also requested a referral to any other agencies that might have cold cases that may need help.

Over about six months, we helped clear up numerous mysteries for several agencies and built a vast reservoir of trust in the process.

Over the rest of my cadaver dog handling career, we stayed as busy as we wanted to be. At this writing, I still receive phone calls from agencies requesting my service even though I haven't handled a cadaver dog in over ten years!

Even though your team's situation is likely different, there are many common traits I bet.

Here are several key take-a-ways that may be applicable from my case study along with some other ideas to consider:

- Focus on trust more than awareness – user agencies don't want marketing they want someone who will reliably help them make their problem go away.
- Work while you wait – it takes time, so use your time smartly. Once you know what services create the most value, work tirelessly building your team's knowledge, skills and abilities to provide those services. Keep accurate records of time spent and credentials acquired.
- Consider hosting a mock drill and ask someone from a user-agency to evaluate you. The agency representatives will appreciate the vulnerability and the willingness to be judged by an outside party.
- Reciprocate – you want them to support your services, so go and support theirs. Even it is not part of your core mission, find out what is important to them and support it. Do they need help distributing toys during the holidays? Even if it doesn't involve you getting to wear your uniform or 'fly your team flag,' the agency will remember your selfless service and start to view you as a partner instead of as a vendor.
- Reduce the Barrier to entry – by providing a fact sheet (not a marketing brochure!), a letter of recommendation, a willingness to demonstrate our abilities, and our 24-hour

pager number, I made it easier for them to call my team when they had a problem that we knew how to solve.

- Understand the prospective agency's reluctance and address it head-on. *"Yes, we're all volunteers that have other jobs. We're also highly trained in these areas and dedicated to serving under your direction to help you solve your problem."*

- Treat them as a customer, not a competitor – Sometimes, a volunteer response team is run by volunteers that, frankly, may know more about how to respond to the event than the responsible agency. That's not an invite to 'rub the agency's nose in it' however by publicly or privately trying to embarrass them for the perceived lack of prowess.
    - If you hired an electrician and they poked fun at you for not knowing how to fix your flux capacitor, would you ever hire that electrician again?
    - When that condition exists, that may provide the perfect opening to provide free training on your response specialty to that agency.
    - If a level of trust is present and they don't feel like you will try to embarrass their status as your student, it may further strengthen you as their partner instead of their vendor.
    - The user-agency is your team's external customer, not the public. Treat them like that within reason, address their reasonable needs, and support their objectives.

Lastly, I don't have to tell you to *not ever, ever show up to an event without an invite, right?*

Millennial Engagement

There's no greater lightning-rod to illustrate the "lack of engagement" than the generation labeled "Millennials." In fact, I initially developed the TEAM Solutions Wheel of Engagement™ to reconcile some of the issues surrounding the surge of Millennials entering the workforce. Let's take another quick look, and then we'll apply it to this unique generation:

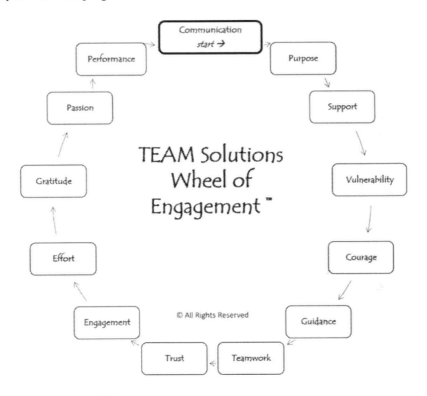

Who are Millennials?

If you're out in public and you look at the person to your left and then look at the person to your right, there's a pretty good chance at least one of them is a Millennial.

- They are young adults, born between 1982 and 2004.
- In 2017, they made up 38% of the workforce.
- By 2020 they will make up 50% of the workforce.

And like those that were labeled Gen X-ers and Baby Boomer's before them, Millennials are here to stay.

So why are Millennials such a hot topic?

Because many of their behaviors are inconsistent with:

1. Expectations and experiences of seniors with Generation X (age 35-50) and Baby Boomer (age 51-69) labels
2. Requirements of the modern workplace

Each generation had its own set of environmental conditions which, depending on your perspective, were either good or bad.

For example, people (from any generation) that had to work long hours with no breaks expect that others should be able to do the same.

When the other person can't (or doesn't) work as hard, resentment grows.

And once resentment starts growing, it's hard to stop.

The modern workplace is full of expectations, and we accuse many Millennials of not making the grade.

Here are some of the behaviors and attitudes often associated with Millennials:

1. Entitled
2. Lazy
3. Selfish
4. Poor work ethic
5. Non-conforming
6. Mentally soft
7. Argumentative
8. Short attention
9. Impatient

Looks familiar? They should. Every generation has people with those behaviors.

Why do Millennials behave that way?

This inescapable truth is this: "we can only do what we're trained to do."

And Millennials are a sum of their training ... just like the rest of us.

Here's what's influenced their training, so far:

Upbringing

Family, school, sports, social media, all reward non-performance (likes, trophies, etc.). Millennials are seldom required to develop coping skills to manage rejection or friction.

Winning is awesome, no doubt about it.

Because it's become socially acceptable to guarantee a reward after every activity, winning becomes the expected result. And the thought of losing fades into the distance. On the surface, that seems justifiable.

However, if we view winning and losing like muscles, the long-term outcomes become more evident and predictable.

When the only muscle that receives a workout is the winning muscle, it will get bigger, hungrier and more expectant.

Similarly, when the 'losing' muscle fails to get any exercise it atrophies and exposes the host (the developing Millennial) to injury.

Over time, the Millennial only knows what it feels like to win and be rewarded. As a result, those same Millennials only have an underdeveloped or even non-existent understanding of how to cope with losing.

Once on their own, facing one of life's inevitable challenges, disappointments, and loss, the Millennial has no coping experience to draw on.

Life Challenge = 1
Millennial = 0

Digital Device Dependency

Devices that replace human interaction with superficial interaction and acceptance are changing how they interact with others. Similar to other addictions!

Like winning, today's digital devices are also awesome.

With our smartphones, we can watch movies, see the weather in Stadt, play games with someone in Hoboken and share picture and experiences instantly with the tap of a button.

With our digital assistants, we can order a roll of toilet paper, play a song or automate our house.

The stuff we used to only be able to do by talking to an actual person can now be done remotely, using a chat box and by simply 'liking' the interaction.

Efficient, yes.

Helpful in building the social skills needed to navigate a multi-generational business, no.

These superficial interactions form the basis of how Millennials (and others) define social acceptance and self-esteem.

- With enough "likes," self-esteem is high. Similar to having enough alcohol, drugs or gambling for an addict.
- Without enough "like," self-esteem is low. Similar to not having enough alcohol, drugs or gambling for an addict.

The problem is real. As with anyone with an untreated addiction, consequences can be enormous.

Instant Gratification

Everything is consumable now, no waiting skills required.

> PLUS: Everybody wants to look from the top of the ladder, but not everyone wants to do the climb.

When the TV show Seinfeld first came out, if you weren't in front of the TV on Thursday night when it came on, you had to wait until the summer to try and catch the re-run.

Now, you can watch every episode in any order you wish, on-demand.

Opportunities for instant gratification are all around us. And similar to our winning and losing muscles our patience muscle is underdeveloped.

As you see, Millennials have acquired their behaviors and attitudes honestly (and predictably).

Real World of Work

When these behaviors and attitudes show up in the workplace, they're not a good fit, even if their knowledge level is. Organizations run by older generations try to force them into THEIR outdated organizational model.

Therefore, there's shared blame when they don't succeed.

For emphasis, let that sink in: *There is blame to share - and responsibility - when they don't succeed.*

This premise is a departure from the popular explanation of the Millennial's lackluster contributions: blaming the Millennial.

Remember: somebody parented, raised, educated and coached the Millennial. These mentors all had a role in creating the person that shows up at our door trying to understand why the copier isn't touch screen and demanding a different color bean bag for their office.

When the Millennial doesn't sit in a meeting without checking their Twitter feed every 2 minutes, perhaps it's because they haven't received proper training on their expected meeting etiquette.

Or, just as likely, they've modeled their behavior after a Gen X-er that does the same thing?

No matter how we slice it, these Millennial frailties and deficiencies are our problem almost as much as it is their problem. The good news is that if we allow someone to be trained to be a non-contributor, we can also train someone to be a contributor.

Like most organizational challenges, the fix starts at the top with the highest levels of modelled leadership.

After recognizing the root of the problem, they must first adjust their attitudes about Millennials to reflect the world's realities where they live, not the world where they want to live.

The way to help a Millennial become a contributing member of an organization is by using the same two methods we use for cultivating any new member:

1. **Training** (*behavior*)
2. **Education** (*attitude*)

The role of proper Training should be self-evident.

- Plumbers learn to plumb stuff.
- Soccer players learn to play soccer.

- Firefighters learn to put the wet stuff on the red stuff, etc.

However, to overcome the complexities of Millennials in the workplace, we need to dig a little deeper.

When I attended elementary school, I was assigned to be a mentor to a new student that had arrived from a foreign land.

Specifically, I was to shepherd him through the school with me and demonstrate what we do when the bell rings, what we do and don't do at recess, how to stand in the lunch line, etc.

He spoke very little English and had some other peculiarities that were both humorous and intriguing.

He was a smart guy, but he never learned how to eat with a fork. Not ever. He'd never even seen one before.

And therein was my first of my many, many lessons in what I call the *"mission within the mission."*

Separately in this program, we've talked about the difference between transactional leadership and transformational leadership.

We often focus (or are told to focus) on all of the little transactions that make up a successful day. For my new classmate, it was how to respond to the school bell, etc. He needed that of course, but his transformation also needed a move from a utensil-free strategy that worked well in his homeland to eating a plate of mashed potatoes with a fork.

We were all ready to help him walk to class, yet few of us were prepared to understand and deliver on the 'mission within the mission".

Millennials and any other new team member have similarities.

1. They come to us knowing X.
2. We are expected to teach them, onboard them, cultivate them to learn X + Y.
3. We discover that what they need is S+N+P+L (Stuff Not Previously Learned) + X + Y.

As has been discussed at length already, Millennials are usually quite smart. They're quite educated, creative and in many cases driven by a purpose, even if it's not your purpose, yet.

Along the way, they also missed out on building a solid foundation of skill in things like:

1. Coping when things don't go well.
2. Accepting rejection.
3. Being patient.
4. Navigating complex social situations.
5. Embracing a moment or two without technology.
6. Adapting to a culture different than their own.
7. Meeting workplace norms.
8. 1-on-1 relationship building.
9. Being successful, not just 'social-media-successful.'
10. Delivering and being appreciated for real effort.

For these Millennials to be successful, heck to even be operational, these skills gaps absolutely must be filled in.

Think of it as advanced onboarding.

One of the most effective ways is through focused and conscientious mentoring and coaching.

Mentoring can help them do things such as connect their "why" to your organization's "why."

Other tactics to help successfully integrate Millennials into the organization:

- Reward effort, not achievement.
  - *"Good effort on the Penske file!"* instead of *"Penske hired us because of you!"*
- Teach and then require workplace etiquette.
  - *"For this meeting to be successful, everyone needs to focus on the conversation. Therefore, all mobile phones are to be left outside or turned completely off. The receptionist has been notified to interrupt any of us in the case of an emergency. Let's begin ..."*

- Create opportunities for small wins AND small losses.
    - We do what we are trained to do.
    - When they win, they shouldn't expect a party.
    - When they lose, they shouldn't expect a whipping.
    - Winning and losing is part of life, and learning how best to respond to these life events is necessary.
- Facilitate 1-on-1 interactions to strengthen in-person social skills.
    - Accompany them to a professional networking group.
    - Have them mentor someone else.
- Build on their existing strengths.
    - Assign them research or another task that takes advantage of their extensive education
    - Include them in brainstorming sessions to maximize their unique perspective.
    - Provide authentic opportunities for them to unify their purpose with your organization's purpose.

Missions are made to accomplish. Even though the hill to overcome with Millennials can be steep at times, it is a hill worth climbing and a mission worth conquering.

Team Engagement

"At this year's event, to empty our inventory and maximize our brand's awareness, we will have two booths that sell t-shirts. One booth will be on the north end of the facility run by Mark, and the other will be on the south end run my Cathy. Whichever person sells the most t-shirts by the end of the event will win a $100 gift card. Cathy and Mark, gather your tribes and get to work!"

Sound familiar? Intra-team contests go on all of the time.

As we tell our kids, competition is great and breeds excellence, right?

The upside of these competitions is well documented:

- T-shirts or whatever get sold in record numbers.
- The winner treats themselves to something nice with their gift card.

The downside gets much less attention though:

- The simmering distrust between the two teams.
- The maneuvering for relevancy goes up while teamwork goes down.

Promoting competition within an organization also creates 'tribalistic tendencies.'

Let's remember that by their very nature, tribes:

- distrust other tribes
- don't share with other tribes and
- may even shoot them with an arrow if they had the chance!

Tribes are certainly good for roving and ravaging the landscape looking for food, but not-so-good for building a high-functioning, intra-organizational team.

In the briefing, the leader offered the WHAT (sell t-shirts) and the WHY (increase brand awareness and empty inventory). So, what would happen if Cathy hit a snag (pardon the pun) with selling her t-shirts and needed Mark's help? Because they're competing, Mark is less likely to help Cathy, which means that Cathy will probably sell fewer shirts. Which means that the objective to sell shirts to increase brand awareness and empty the inventory is now less likely to happen. Who's the winner and the loser now?

Whenever competition increases, teamwork decreases.

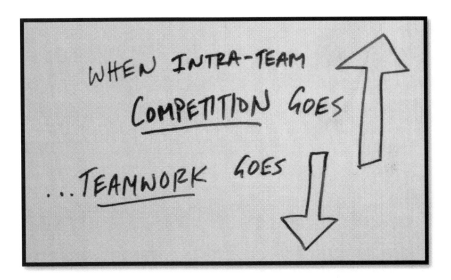

Similarly, when one person on a 'team' is the sole decision maker, teamwork tends to go down as engagement and competition for relevancy go up.

What about the people Mark had helping him at his booth, wouldn't they want to share in the gift card too? If Mark were the only one in his booth making decisions about how and where to sell the t-shirts, the helpers would be less likely to work together since they would instead be maneuvering to be recognized by Mark.

Again, whenever competition increases, teamwork decreases.

Do you want to have a high-functioning team? Drop the intra-organizational competition.

"My loyalty to country and team is beyond reproach. I humbly serve as a guardian to my fellow Americans, always ready to defend those who are unable to defend themselves. I do not advertise the nature of my work, nor seek recognition for my actions. I voluntarily accept the inherent hazards of my profession, placing the welfare and security of others before my own. I serve with honor on and off the battlefield. The ability to control my emotions and my actions, regardless of circumstance, sets me apart from other men. ... In the absence of orders, I will take charge, lead my teammates and accomplish the mission. ... I will never quit. I persevere and thrive on adversity. My nation expects me to be physically harder and mentally stronger than my enemies. If knocked down, I will get back up, every time. I will draw on every remaining ounce of strength to protect my teammates and to accomplish our mission. I am never out of the fight." ~ U.S. Navy SEALs Creed

SUMMARY – TEAM Solutions Wheel of Engagement™

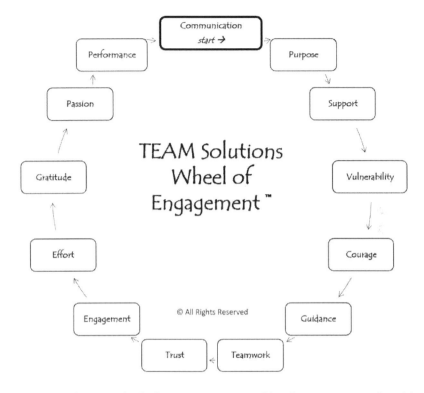

The TEAM Solutions Wheel of Engagement™ provides the Response Leader with a consistent framework to transform themselves and others into highly engaged and productive team members.

The framework is appropriate for the new team member who's learning what the organization stands for or the veteran team member who has grown disillusioned, disengaged, and disgruntled.

As a wheel with no definitive beginning or end, there's a tendency to start the Wheel of Enagagement™ at the step where the team member's engagement level starts to fade.

While you will ultimately decide how best to engage your team, I recommend starting with "Communication" to ensure that each subsequent action builds on a solid foundation created by the previous step.

Let's summarize each step of the TEAM Solutions Wheel of Engagement™:

1. **Communication** – *Deliver clear and accurate objectives, strategies, and tactics (P.O.S.T.), as appropriate.*
2. **Purpose** – *Answer the "why" question and provide necessary details.*
3. **Support** – *Communicate how, where, and when the team member can receive needed support. Encourage the team member to ask for support and then provide it without judgment.*
4. **Vulnerability** – *Facilitate team member's admission of feeling vulnerable. Explore what would make a positive difference for the team member.*
5. **Courage** – *Reinforce the team member's courage to speak up even when feeling vulnerable.*
6. **Guidance** – *Provide clear and helpful support so the team member can experience the positive difference.*
7. **Teamwork** – *Arrange for and encourage authentic and productive support from other team members.*
8. **Trust** – *Connect the Guidance and Teamwork as the result of the team member's Vulnerability and Courage so the team member can build trust.*
9. **Engagement** – *Create opportunities for the team member to engage with the Purpose.*
10. **Effort** – *Recognize team member's effort and their contribution to the overall team.*
11. **Gratitude** – *Express thanks publicly while providing an appropriate reward (tangible or intangible) for the team member's contributions to the organization's success.*
12. **Passion** – *Reinforce the enthusiasm that the team member now exemplifies.*
13. **Performance** – *Acknowledge and celebrate a higher performing team member and organization.*

To keep your organization and the team members that comprise it performing, keep the TEAM Solutions Wheel of Engagement™ spinning.

Forecasting

Your D.U.F.F.E.L. B.A.G.:

1. Developing
2. Unifying
3. ***Forecasting***
4. Funding
5. Equipping
6. Learning
7. Boosting
8. Assessing
9. Getting Ready to Act

"Planning is bringing the future into the present so that you can do something about it now." ~ *Alan Lakein*

Forecasting is an essential element for a Response Leader to possess. And like a muscle, the ability to forecast successfully improves the more it gets a workout.

A forecast represents the best guess, based on the best input, from the best planners doing their best work and aiming for their best result.

However, even with all of that effort, forecasts are seldom 100% accurate. Ever watch a spring weather forecast in North Texas?

When, not if a forecast does not come to fruition, most consider it great sport to ridicule, cajole and embarrass the forecaster. Like when perennial losers the Cleveland Browns are forecast to win a Super Bowl. Easy to poke fun, but it can underscore the challenges of accurate forecasting.

To make a clear distinction, forecasting things like winning lottery numbers, next year's Kentucky Derby winner and other games of chance are not the forecasting skill I'm referring to here.

Forecasting using sound metrics, logic, and critical decision-making is where the Response Leader shines.

"Long-range planning does not deal with future decisions, but with the future of present decisions." ~ Peter Drucker

---

Forecasts typically result in one of two different conditions:

1. Forecasting something not-so-favorable will happen
2. Forecasting something favorable will happen

However, to a Response Leader, the result of the forecast is not nearly as important as the knowledge needed to make more informed decisions.

Therefore, both favorable and unfavorable conditions should be captured to help drive event objectives forward.

Example:

Forecast = rain
Objective = pack an umbrella

Forecast = increased sales
Objective = plan for an increase in staff and inventory

Furthermore, if the input produces an unpleasant forecast, we can sometimes change the input to improve the forecast.

Example:

Input = current response training activity is underdeveloped
Forecast = lack of Readiness to Act

New Input = relevant, scheduled and supervised response training 2x per month

New Forecast = improved Readiness to Act

Of course, this cause-and-effect modeling may not seem very revolutionary, yet a shocking number of organizations fail to put even basic effort into forecasting.

The most impactful forecasts deal with disruptions and other unpleasant conditions. Things like cyber-breaches, natural disasters, criminal activity, etc. so the rest of this topic will focus on ways to forecast not only what threats lurk in the night but also what to do about them.

Collectively, this body of knowledge is called contingency planning.

Contingency Planning

We plan in the sunshine to operate in the storm. What storms lie ahead?

"One of the true tests of leadership is the ability to recognize a problem before it becomes an emergency." ~ Arnold H. Glasow

---

After 20+ years of responding to natural and human-made disruptions (tornadoes, hurricanes, murders, suicides, crime scenes, etc.) a few common traits emerged among leaders I've worked with:

We're all imperfect people ...
performing an imperfect task ...
in an imperfect environment.

Therefore, expecting perfection under these conditions is a fool's game.

So, by knowing that our event (planned or unplanned) will be imperfect, we can more readily embrace the need to anticipate and address what can and will go wrong.

It bears repeating:

"If it's predictable, it's preventable."

What about the "worst case scenario"? These catastrophes are what inspire the news headlines: the world is ending, the stock market is crashing, the people are dying from poison, etc.

However, most assume that "it can never happen to me" because that scenario is unlikely.

Worst case though is about consequence, not probability.

Therefore, planning must include both consequence AND probability.

If you've been following me for any length of time you've likely heard me grouse about "proportional risk management," i.e., keeping your risk proportional to the reward or upside of the activity.

Not surprisingly, most of us are addressing the wrong thing, and as a result, our actual risk doesn't go down at all. Oops.

In his short YouTube video called *"What Kills Us? How We Understand Risk,"* Dr. Aaron E. Carroll of Healthcare Triage illustrates these irrational approaches perfectly.

Example:

In 2001 the American Academy of Pediatrics (AAP) promoted a policy that all children under the age of two must sit in a safety seat while traveling in an airplane. The existing policy allows young children to ride on a parent's lap. The AAP policy would require purchasing a separate seat for the child instead and require the logistics of traveling with a child safety seat.

When researchers studied the impact of the policy more closely, they determined that:

- Less than one child airplane death would be prevented per year at the cost of $1.3 Billion for the prevention (extra plane seats purchased at an average of $200 each.)

- Nearly 20% of the traveling families would not pay for an extra plane seat, choosing to drive to their destination instead.
- Statistically, driving instead of flying would drastically increase child deaths. Nearly 1000 children per year die in car accidents.
- If you had to choose between a policy that could cause one child death or choose a policy that could cause 1000 child deaths, what would you do?

Using an ill-informed and fear-based policy to push children from a better place (less-risky airplane sitting in a parent's lap) to a worse place (more-risky ground transportation) fails to consider consequence and probability.

More data from Dr. Carroll:

Accidents, including car accidents, are the leading cause of death in children, causing nearly 1600 deaths per year.

Alarmingly, to me at least, the second and third leading causes of death in children and young adults is suicide and homicide. In adults, heart disease outpaces all cancers, strokes, and respiratory issues combined as the leading cause of death in adult men and women. Even with statistical fluctuations and imperfections, the data is compelling.

However, when we look at the 'death prevention landscape,' we see a disproportionate focus on different cancers and children dying in airplanes instead of mental health and heart disease.

Information is available to develop risk reduction strategies; we just have to be willing to look through its imperfections and take action.

Now, let's look more closely at risk for strategies to be less imperfect.

Risk Assessment 101

Risk Formula

To calculate risk, Response Leaders use the following formula and definitions:

Threat + Vulnerability + Likelihood + Consequence = Risk

Threat/Hazard = *what we're trying to protect ourselves from*
Vulnerability = *weakness or gap in protecting ourselves from it*
Likelihood = *the chance that the threat will occur*
Consequence = *the impact of the threat occurring*
=
Risk – *The potential for damage or loss due to the threat*

Example:

When my daughter was little, she was afraid of being bitten by a shark. A rational fear perhaps for someone who washes their dishes in the surf of Australia's beaches but not for a little girl living in the Desert Southwest of the United States.

By assigning each component a number value of 1 out 10 (10 being the worst), the math problem looked like this:

Threat = *shark bite*
Vulnerability of being bitten by a shark while living in a desert = 0
Likelihood of a shark bite occurring in the desert = 0
The **consequence** of a shark biting her if she encountered one = 2 (if a shark were in the desert, biting my daughter would be the least of their concerns!)

Therefore, her **Risk** of being eaten by a shark was very *low*. That's despite what the producers of "Shark Week" may suggest.

Now consider the risks associated with an outdoor tournament being held during a weekend in early May in North Texas (where I live).

Threat = tornado disrupting outdoor tournament in May
Vulnerability of a tornado being harmful to those exposed outdoors = 9
Likelihood = 8 (an average of 44 tornadoes impact Texas every May)
Consequence = 10 (while they may not always tear down houses, they will certainly impact every outdoor activity in its path)

Therefore, the **RISK** of a tornado disrupting a North Texas outdoor tournament in May is *high*.

Recognizing any activity that has the potential to become a 'patient generator' must receive focused attention!

By knowing when this potential exists, our situational awareness is high, and the chance of making a successful, well-informed decision is also high.

In government, risk assessments are sometimes called a "THIRA," or Threat and Hazard Identification and Risk Assessment. Therefore the 'THIRA process' bears mentioning.

THIRA Process

The THIRA (Threat and Hazard Identification and Risk Assessment) process is used extensively by governmental agencies in their community preparedness plans. In part, because having a THIRA in place qualifies them to receive grant money but also because the process is designed to serve an entire community, including the private sector, broadly.

To that end, all 50 states and any agency that receives Urban Area Security Initiative (UASI) funding are required to conduct a THIRA. A THIRA is encouraged for everyone else.

The process is a common trigger for a community or organization that's enhancing their understanding of what risks they face and what to do about them. By better understanding those risks, they can better perform in each phase of emergency management:

1. **Prevention**
2. **Protection**
3. **Mitigation**
4. **Response**
5. **Recovery**

There are four phases to the THIRA process, which I simplify below:

Phase 1: Identify the Threat/Hazard

These threats and hazards should fall into one of the below categories:

Natural – Earthquakes, hurricanes, floods, tornadoes, locust infestations, etc.

Technological – Train derailment, levee or dam failure, power failures, etc.

Human-made – Cyber-attack, school or workplace violence, explosives attack, etc.

The list should address any threat or hazard that is both likely to occur and significant to the community or organization.

If you were to participate in developing a THIRA, based on likelihood and significance, you'd need to incorporate as many wide-ranging threats and hazards as possible from as many stakeholders and subject matter experts as possible. This outreach is another reason why maintaining relationships across the Response Leader spectrum is valuable.

Phase 2: Put Threats and Hazards into Context

The simplest way to do that is to take the list from Phase 1 and ask some "how" and some "what" questions.

Let's use a train derailment as an example:

1.   *How would the residents, business, etc. in the area impacted fare?*
2.   *How would the train wreck impact our community's ability to operate?*
3.   *How did the community handle the last train wreck?*
4.   *What time of day (or year) would make it worse?*
5.   *What location would a train wreck do more damage?*
6.   *What factors would increase the severity of a train wreck?*

Once each threat and hazard have some 'context,' priorities start to emerge based on their likelihood and estimated impact.

Phase 3: Establish Capability Targets for each Core Capability
Phase 4: Apply the Results

NOTE: Verbiage like that is why I create books and programs like this, by the way!

Essentially, in Phase 3 you make a plan to address the threats and hazards identified in Phase 1, using the priorities that emerged in Phase 2 and put them into action for Phase 4.

The plan should include all of the people and things from the whole community or organization that have a solution to offer. To further our train wreck example, some desired outcomes in our plan might be:

1. Create a multi-agency task force of hazmat technicians, railway experts, traffic engineers and perimeter control that's on-call 24 hours per day.
2. Evacuate the neighborhood downwind of the tracks within 3 hours.
3. Establish shelter for people and pets within 2 hours.
4. Assess the viability of roads and tracks within 6 hours.

As a Response Leader, you have or will experience organizations that rely on a THIRA process (remember what I said about grant money). So even though I don't find it especially intuitive, ideal or in some cases practical, it's important that you're familiar with how and why it exists.

Regardless how the information is derived, assessing the threats and hazards is necessary. And once identified, they need treating.

5 Risk Treatments

Risks can be treated using one of five (5) strategies:

1. **Avoid**
2. **Accept**
3. **Transfer**
4. **Mitigate**
5. **Share**

Using the outdoor sports tournament as an example, here are some risk treatment options to consider:

Avoid the risk - don't host the tournament in May
Accept the risk - host the tournament anyway

Transfer the risk - obtain insurance to cover any losses arising from tornado damage

Mitigate the risk - move the tournament indoors

Share the risk - enter into a shared liability arrangement with another event organizer

If the risks identified in the THIRA are going to be accepted, mitigated or shared, a helpful organizing tool is a Pre-Event Planning Matrix.

Pre-Event Planning Matrix

The Pre-Event Planning Matrix helps you choose the risks, hazards, or functions required by an event, and assigns responsibility for each of them.

Using the simple matrix below or anything similar, add your threats and hazards in the left column and the stakeholders along the top row.

Then follow these three simple steps.

1. Identify the risks, hazards and functional responsibilities for your event.
2. Indicate which agency has primary responsibility for them by adding a "P" in the column.
3. Indicate which agency or agencies have secondary or support responsibility for them by adding an "S" in the column.

Pre-Event Planning Matrix

1. Identify the risks, hazards and functional responsibilities for your event.
2. Indicate which agency has primary responsibility for them by adding a "P" in the column.
3. Indicate which agency or agencies have secondary or support responsibility for them by adding a "S" in the column.

	County Agency	EMS	Emergency Mgmt.	FAA	FBI	Fire Rescue	Law Enforcement	Public Health	Public Works	State Agencies	Secret Service	Public Works	Event Sponsor	Private Security	Vendors	Volunteer Groups			
Abandoned Vehicles																			
Airspace Encroachment																			
Bomb Threat																			
Civil Disturbance																			
Communications (Technology)																			
Communications (Operations)																			
Community Relations																			
Credentials																			
Crowd Control																			
Demonstrations																			

Content modified from DHS/FEMA   Learn more at TEAM-Solutions.US   Page 1 of 4

Obviously, the THIRA process and a Pre-Event Planning Matrix are most useful when used before an event occurs. Even so, going through the steps can offer great insight into what to expect if you get involved later in the response.

After all, knowledge is power!

Categories of Knowledge

When faced with a potential crisis, start with a quick analysis of what information is known to the event planners.

1. *What do we know?*
2. *What do we know that we don't know?*
3. *What don't we know that we don't know?*

These questions and their answers form the basis of our knowledge and allow us to start making sense of the crisis.

In turn, when we start making sense out of the crisis, the quality and accuracy of our decisions improve. And better decisions lead to better outcomes.

Let's look more closely at the different levels of knowledge, using a simple rainstorm as an example.

> "I know that it's raining." (*Things we know that we know*)
> Usually, a simple problem to assess and solve.

> "I don't know if it will be raining tomorrow." (*Things we know that we don't know*)
> A more complicated problem to solve since it requires resourcefulness, experience or analysis.

> "I didn't consider that the rain could turn to ice, cause an accident and power outage and impact my upcoming travel." (*Things we don't know that we don't know*)
> A considerably more complex problem to solve since we don't readily acknowledge that a problem even exists and there may be several, elusive correct solutions.

"Not knowing what we don't know" is sometimes called the **"Red Slice."** I first learned about The Red Slice from my dedicated colleagues that served at the Los Angeles Fire Department and fought daily to reduce the size of their "Red Slice."

> Lastly, for someone just surfacing after living underground their whole life: "What is the wet stuff falling from the sky?" (*Things that we don't even comprehend could exist in the first place*)

This last type of knowledge deficiency can plunge Response Leaders into chaos.

And the solution to chaos is action, not just knowledge. Be sure to be familiar with the section on decision-making for tools to improve your decision-making skills.

Without immediate action, disorder takes over. And disorder can end up being worse than the original crisis.

Response Leaders after the terrorist attacks on 9/11 are an example of all of these:

1. After initial disorder and chaos, they deployed available resources to respond to the emergency because they knew that they knew how to do that.
2. They assembled intelligence sources to gain insight into what happened because they knew that there were things they didn't know.
3. They took immediate action to ground flights, evacuate people, etc. because they didn't know what would happen next.

Making sense out of these dynamic events is no small task. A more advanced method to wrap your head around these chaotic situations is called a Cynefin framework, named by its Welsh innovator and meaning "Habit."

The Cynefin framework essentially categorizes knowledge into five contexts:

1. Simple or Obvious – known knowns
2. Complicated – known unknowns
3. Complex – unknown unknowns
4. Chaotic – paralyzed by inaction
5. Disorder – void of all clarity and knowledge

Remember, knowing something valuable – including the above breakdowns - during a time of chaos is meaningless without decisive action. Therefore, it's essential that Response Leaders understand, practice and constantly improve their decision-making skills to keep the crisis from escalating.

One of the ways Response Leaders predict and prevent something simple from escalating into something chaotic is to promote and maintain "Situational Awareness."

Situational Awareness (SA)

Imagine this:

You're approaching a busy intersection with cars, trucks, and pedestrians whizzing by in all directions.

You start walking through the intersection ...

How is your ability to predict and avoid being hit?

If your head is down, looking at your mobile phone, you have poor situational awareness and a high likelihood of an unpleasant consequence (i.e., you'll get squished).

However, if your head is on a swivel, you see the eyes of the drivers in your midst, and you are predicting which ones pose the greatest risk to your safety then you have good situational awareness.

The amount of situational awareness we have can determine if our event's outcome is successful or not.

Therefore, situational awareness refers to:

1.   Knowing what's around you
2.   Understanding its significance
3.   Anticipating its impact on your current activity

Situational awareness is a 12-dollar word that describes what goes into the decision when you bring an umbrella to your son's soccer match because it might rain.

Simply put:

1.   WITH enough situational awareness you have a greater chance of successfully staying dry.
2.   WITHOUT enough situational awareness you have a greater risk of failing to stay dry.

NOTE: Since its inception as a mental tool used by the US military, the concept of situational awareness (SA) has spawned its own, growing field of study. While SA remains a topic of research by cognitive scientists, my SA references are purely tactical and for everyday use.

Every part of our life benefits from an increase in situational awareness.

Furthermore, maintaining a high degree of situational awareness is the secret weapon to preventing an issue from growing into a crisis.

So let's examine how we can improve our situational awareness.

OODA Loop

OODA is an acronym that stands for its four parts: *Observe, Orient, Decide, Act*

Former US Air Force pilot and military strategist John Boyd developed the OODA Loop model to refine how people and organizations react to an event. In the theatre of war, whoever reacts more quickly usually wins.

1. **Observation**: the collection of data by using all of our senses
2. **Orientation**: the analysis and synthesis of the data to define our current condition
3. **Decision**: the determination of a course of action based on our current condition
4. **Action**: the execution of that decision

Separately we discuss the heuristics of Decision-Making and Taking Action, so I want to focus on the aspects that most directly increase our situational awareness: Observation and Orientation.

Observation

Situational awareness is very much a "garbage in, garbage out" system. If we input lousy data, we tend to get lousy results.

So where do we develop the data input?

Are cars racing toward us while we're crossing the street? Knowing that useful data comes from looking up, looking around and checking over our shoulders.

In a crisis, observations are direct like the above example, or they're indirect. Indirect observations come from sources outside our purview, like from other Response Leaders, subject matter experts, and external sources.

A comprehensive breakdown of the who, what, where, and why of managing the flow of information and observations during an event is discussed later.

There are some notable impediments to developing adequate observations to factor in, also.

- **Attentional narrowing** – this refers to the involuntary narrowing of our peripheral vision. From a normal view of about 190 degrees or 155 degrees per eye, some studies suggest that adults can lose almost 60 degrees of actual horizontal vision and almost 80 degrees of vertical vision during a stressful episode.

When someone develops "tunnel vision" during a challenging time, including as a result of being thrust into a crisis response, that's attentional narrowing.

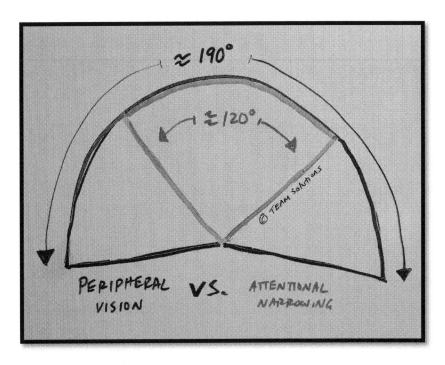

The same dynamic of attentional narrowing applies to our mental processes used in decision-making. Please familiarize yourself with the decision-making models and challenges presented earlier.

To counteract the challenges and to improve our observation, rely on awareness and practice.

Observation by walking around (OBWA). OBWA is an adaptation of the management style of "managing by wandering around," except designed for observation and increasing situational awareness.

Out of all of the Response Leaders that I've seen on actual events and in training, the most insightful ones have these two characteristics:

1. They frequently walk around observing what is happening.
2. They have the equivalent of one hand in their pocket and other on a cup of coffee, a behavior indicating that they're present to watch and listen, not meddle.

Practice, practice, practice. Whenever plausible, challenge yourself to notice the un-noticeable by asking yourself (or your partner, colleague, etc.) some "what," "where, " "when," and "how" type questions.

- How many people in the restaurant have long hair?
- Where are the exits in the theatre? (You already do this, I know)
- Was that car here before?
- What's the current mood or vibe of this place?
- How high was the water line this morning?
- How many people self-reported to the hospital today?

Becoming a skilled observer takes effort and practice. Even then, observations are not very helpful unless we put them in the proper context.

Orientation

Now that we have a shelf full of observations, what do we do with them?

Like the previous discussion about the THIRA process, providing context for our observations sets us up favorably for decisive action.

However, unlike a THIRA process which identifies dynamic threats and hazards, we want to establish a static baseline with our observations for context.

From there, variances to our baseline will be more identifiable and therefore more actionable, sooner.

Example:

- If the water level rises above the curb (baseline), you'll be primed to notice and take action.
- If the guy that was sitting quietly (baseline) now starts pacing or acting erratically after the police officer leaves, you'll be primed to notice and take action.
- If the typical admittance rate of people self-reporting to the hospital (baseline) increases, you'll be primed to notice and take action.

When I teach technical search & rescue with cameras and listening devices, establishing a baseline is also critical.

For example, a person trapped under a pile of rubble may be unconscious and covered in concrete dust and debris. It's incredibly difficult to recognize and identify what is or is not a person (identifiable face and hands, for example) in those conditions. Therefore, successfully locating them requires looking for anomalies like the rounded edges of a human shape (anomaly) versus the expected sharp edges of a building collapse (baseline).

Establishing baselines and scanning for anomalies are major factors for success for anybody, including Response Leaders.

Just having the information and the proper context is not enough. Remember, knowledge without action is meaningless during a crisis.

Accessing the database of mental models that we discussed earlier will bring clarity to the Decision-making and the Action phases of the OODA Loop.

So far, this discussion has centered around only one person having the observations, the findings, and the context.

However, if an event begins to escalate, possessing accurate and timely information becomes even more critical.

But, *who else needs to know that information?*

Common Operating Picture (COP)

A common trap is to receive information but to let it die a sad, lonely death before ensuring that the right people know it, too.

<u>For example:</u>

Some among you may remember when everyone had home phones and nobody had cell phones. To call and talk to the cute girl from class, I called her home number only to have my call screened by her little sister who offered to take a message. Except her younger sister failed to pass along the message that I called. At school the next day, I was jilted that the girl of my affection didn't acknowledge my call and she, in turn, was jilted because she thought I never called in the first place. Neither one of us was operating with a common operating picture.

A more relevant example is when responders grouse about 'poor communication' during their After-Action Report. The failure to maintain an adequate common operating picture is a big, underlying reason why.

That's why a common operating picture is needed to avoid breaking or slowing the flow of critical information.

<u>Example:</u>

Ruth smelled the gas and saw all of the panicked workers who noticed it by accident in front of the business. However, she did not notify her colleagues in the back of the business, who required hospitalization after being overcome by gas fumes.

"Who else needs to know this?" is a common question Response Leaders ask themselves to promote a common operating picture.

Two of my favorite methods to promote a common operating picture are by:

1. displaying a large, constantly updated master map of the event
2. maintaining robust, easily consumable and understandable notes on a whiteboard

I've been in or worked in several dozen emergency operations centers around the country with high-tech display screens, software, and monitors.

For people that will be working in the same room, however, believe me when I tell you that those displays don't hold a candle to a simple whiteboard and a big wall map.

If you're planning on enhancing your war room, ops center, etc., I encourage you to dedicate ample wall space for whiteboards and maps.

By default, every Response Leader must encourage everyone in the organization to ask these two questions to improve their COP:

1. When possessing information ask: **"Who else needs to know this?"**
2. When needing information ask: **"Who has that information?"**

Rinse and repeat until everyone is asking those two questions on auto-pilot.

So, how do we know when we have achieved a common operating picture?

Unfortunately, a common operating picture is not all that common. Gaps are commonplace, especially due to the dynamic nature of many crises. However, by training, communicating, and modeling COP best practices, these gaps are manageable.

Sometimes the event requires the services of an organized incident management team full of Response Leaders. The Incident Command System (ICS) framework that they'll use makes accommodation for a common operating picture through the activation of a Situation Unit Leader, or SITL.

What's the Situation Unit's purpose? To actively gather and display an up-to-date status of all relevant event information.

Since the Situation Unit plays such an integral role in a Response Leader's success, an entire section is dedicated to them later.

Business Impact Analysis (BIA)

In the private sector, most progressive companies that want to avoid the ill-effects of a disruption conduct a Business Impact Analysis, or BIA.

A BIA is essentially the enhanced application of the below risk formula:

Threat + Vulnerability + Likelihood + Consequence = Risk

Threat/Hazard = what we're trying to protect ourselves from
Vulnerability = weakness or gap in protecting ourselves from it
Likelihood = the chance that the threat will occur
Consequence = the impact of the threat occurring
=
Risk – The potential for damage or loss due to the threat

Instead of one or two informed Response Leaders conducting a risk assessment, BIA's are intended to be more comprehensive and applicable to every facet of the organization.

Therefore, when Response Leaders perform a BIA, they commonly distribute a questionnaire to their organization's segmented departments, divisions, and functions for them to report on the subtle and not-so-subtle impacts that a disruption would cause them.

Example:

If Acme Printing had to evacuate their facility due to a gas leak (an identified threat), the sales staff might identify that their paper vendor - who only delivers 1x per month - could miss making a delivery. The resulting supply chain disruption could cause subsequent disruptions to the overall organization's ability to fill and collect their customer's orders.

Identifying these not-always-obvious dependencies requires awareness and effort on the part of the Response Leader. That's why it's advisable to perform and keep updated a thorough Business Impact Analysis long before it's needed.

Of course, you don't have to be a business to use a BIA; the process is valuable whenever there is a chance for disruption.

There are multiple guidelines and compliance standards for BIA's available from business continuity trade groups, FEMA, etc.

Continuity of Operations Plan (COOP)

Mother nature doesn't discriminate between the public and private sector when she wreaks havoc.

If an EF4 tornado rips down Main Street, the private sector accounting office and the public-sector clerk's office face the same risk of a disruption.

A Continuity Of Operations Plan (COOP) is similar to a Business Impact Analysis (BIA) that the private sector uses to identify risks to their business.

For a COOP, the public-sector agency evaluates and plans for essential services that must continue to operate, like fire and EMS response, regardless of the disruption.

There are nine total components that a Response Leader addresses in a successful COOP plan:

1. **Essential services** - police, fire, EMS, etc.
2. **Succession plan** - in the event agency leaders are not available.
3. **Authority to delegate** – in the absence of regular lines of authority.
4. **Alternate facilities** - used to carry out essential functions.
5. **Communications** - in support of essential functions.
6. **Vital Records Management** – protection of critical electronic and hard-copy documents.
7. **Human Resource Support** - for employees and agents during a disruption.
8. **Transfer of authority** - to agencies not affected.
9. **Recovery** - of all primary functions.

By contrast, a private sector business is not typically required to operate so they may close their doors until the threat goes away.

Developing a COOP is critical (and usually required) for public sector agencies but not relevant for most private sector organizations.

Pre-Mortem

Anytime we are faced with a decision that produces an uncertain future; we can ask our brain trust of associates:

"If this event fails, what will be the reason?"

Forcing everyone to predict and creatively kill the event before it even begins produces incredible insight.

And from that insight can come incredible contingency planning to prevent the failure.

Nothing says success like killing your project before even starting it, right?

<u>Picture this:</u>

You assemble your brain trust around the table to launch your next, big initiative. Saving the rain forest, responding to a disaster, overhauling the tax code, whatever.

You – as the mindful leader – offer your high-level view of the HOW, the WHY, the WHEN, etc. And then you ask for and receive thunderous support.

Sometime later everyone is seated at the same table, head in hands, trying to figure out why the initiative failed so spectacularly.

Then "Jason" pipes up from the back of the room: *"well, I could have told you THAT was going to happen!"*

Grrr.

The Project Premortem provides a simple way to avoid thumping "Jason" in the head.

Unlike the postmortem exam we perform on dead people and things to figure out how they died, a premortem is, you guessed it, just the opposite.

Now picture this:

Same meeting, same project, same people (including "Jason").

You – the mindful leader – after delivering the project overview ask:

"If this project fails, what will be the reason?"

"Now pair up, take 5 minutes and report your findings."

This query provides "Jason's" moment to shine: *"It will fail because nobody is using a VHS player anymore, duh!"* (or similar insight, of course)

Voilà.

Now you have more insight and forecasting from a collective brain trust by which you can make a more informed decision and reduce the chance of project failure.

So, when you can ask *"Can everyone support this plan?"* You'll get informed nods in return.

One piece of interesting backstory is how some of the Stoic philosophers (Marcus Aurelius, Seneca, and Epictetus) also practiced pre-mortems. Except they called them "premeditatio malorum," which translates to a "premeditation of evils."

Similarly, a strategy of inversion or starting at the opposite end was embraced by the German mathematician Carl Jacobi. He used the mindset of "man muss immer umkehren" or, "invert, always invert" to solve vexing problems.

Aside from the history lesson, how does this help a Response Leader in the heat of a battle?

By understanding and equipping ourselves with this pre-mortem, inversion strategy, we can better avoid friction and failure.

Here's an example from a recent conversation with my son:

Me: *"What would make Mom upset?"*

Son: *"Leaving my socks and shoes on the floor in the living room."*

Me: (waits for that pre-mortem to settle in)

Son: Picks up shoes and socks.

From a more risk intensive environment, like a disaster response:

Response Leader #1: *"What would make the conditions for our disaster victims worse?"*

Response Leader #2: *"Taking them from their damaged home (bad place) and putting them on an unsheltered overpass with no food, water, or hygiene facility (worse place)."*

Response Leader #1: *"Right. Let's make sure if we move them that it's a move to a better place, not to a worse place."*

From a more static environment inside an organization:

"What would an arrogant supervisor do in this situation?"

(Hint: do the inverse!)

Inverting the problem, killing it in advance, premeditating evil or simply beginning with the end in mind all are hallmarks of a world-class Response Leader.

Loss Aversion

A notable mental model that impacts Response Leaders is called "Loss Aversion," which describes a mindset where one would rather avoid a loss than increase that chance to win.

When deciding how to manage a risky investment in the stock market, this is an easy metric to evaluate.

But, what about deciding whether to send people toward a dangerous area to save lots of people, or wait until the danger subsides to save a few people? Evaluating this is much more difficult.

In nearly every response there is an assumption of risk and an expectation of safety. That presents a vexing challenge for the Response Leader that needs reconciling.

Begin by identifying where you are on the 'loss aversion scale' in other areas of your life.

For example:

Do you act in a way that minimizes the chance of losing your golf game?

or

Do you act in a way that maximizes your chance of winning?

By knowing what your mental models predispose you to do, you'll make a more informed and clear decision about potential loss versus potential gain.

These are not the only tools you'll need to lead the troops into battle, but they can sure reduce your casualties.

Due to coordination, training, and expense, some aspects of risk reduction are difficult to achieve. On the other hand, some aspects are in our control, like maintaining an adequate balance between work and rest.

Work / Rest Cycles

For both planned and unplanned events there's a hidden imbalance that threatens most of us:

Work / Rest cycles

Even with proper planning, Response Leaders may allow themselves to be overworked and under-rested.

Yes, Response Leaders should set an example to others about diligence and mental toughness.

However, Response Leaders should also set the example for the benefits that come from being balanced and well-rested.

That example includes creating plans that incorporate sensible rest cycles and not just plans that focus on relentless work cycles.

The downside is notable:

- Studies conducted and duplicated several times have measured the mental acuity and motor skills of experienced drivers, medics and military personnel who had been awake for between 17-19 hours.
- On average, their response speeds were 50% slower.
- In tests of their motor skills, their performance was equivalent to a person with a blood-alcohol level of .10 (over the legal limit of blood alcohol).

The point is clear: *Without proper rest, you're endangering yourself and the people and events around you.* Either through unsafe actions or deficient decision-making.

Since the lack of rest is predictable, it is also preventable.

The Response Leadership Sequence™ has peaks of high activity and demands on a Response Leaders time, specific to the role they're performing.

So, steps to create a balance between work and rest consist of:

1. Rest during non-peak time should be identified, scheduled and protected to allow for a Response Leader to rejuvenate.
2. When possible, define tasks that accommodate a reasonable work/rest cycle. (i.e., instead of "dig a hole to China" say "Over the next 4 hours, dig a hole to China, then report back with your progress")
3. Schedule resources around the time they have to be there, plus preparation time at the beginning and time for decompression/rehabilitation at the end. For example, if you don't need them until noon, don't have them arrive at 6 am, just because that is when you get there.
4. DO NOT send resources home unless and until they receive an adequate rest and rehabilitation period, first!

With a little bit of forethought and a little leadership, you can reverse the trend of poor work/rest management.

SUMMARY – Contingency Planning

There were several contingency planning methods discussed. Response leaders use some of them or all of them to proceed uninterrupted through the Sequence of Response™.

- Risk Assessment and THIRA
- Categories of Knowledge
- Situational Awareness (SA)
- Common Operating Picture (COP)
- Business Impact Analysis (BIA)
- Continuity of Operations Plan (COOP)
- Pre-Mortem
- Work / Rest Cycles

Hurricane Katrina (2005) provides another helpful example which underscores the importance of contingency planning.

- Most people in New Orleans knew something could go wrong.
- Some of them prepared for something to go wrong (stored food/water, saw to cut themselves out of their attic, etc.)
- Fewer of them were Ready to Act.

Being Ready to Act is one of the chief difference-makers between a victim and a survivor and is a hallmark of all capable Response Leaders.

Funding

Your D.U.F.F.E.L. B.A.G.:

1. Developing
2. Unifying
3. Forecasting
4. ***Funding***
5. Equipping
6. Learning
7. Boosting
8. Assessing
9. Getting Ready to Act

Sometimes the financial support needed to develop and respond to an event are conceived, grown and implemented with fairy dust; but most often real money is required to 'lubricate' the operation.

When I was in the product security business, I investigated instances of both cargo theft and counterfeiting of major, internationally known consumer brands.

The counterfeit issue of inferior and sometimes dangerous products that illegally bore these company's names and logos was a much wider spread problem than stealing trailer loads of the real thing.

So, which initiative received more funding?

Cargo theft. Because it's measurable in a quantifiable and qualifiable way, it's easier for finance folks to see the impact of their funding decision.

"2 tractor trailer loads of brand name shirts were stolen yesterday at noon. The cost of those items was 400 thousand dollars."

vs.

"There was a reported sighting of someone selling counterfeit watches bearing our trademark on it at the flea market."

The contents of the stolen trailer were a direct impact on the company because they were destined to stores that, once sold, would net the company much more than 400 thousand dollars. The opportunity for the company to sell those shirts disappeared along with the stolen trailer.

Even if we established that the flea market vendor was the tip of a criminal enterprise that counterfeited those watches around the country, the loss to the company was indirect. Those counterfeit watches didn't directly displace a sale, so it was harder to justify funding the effort to stop them.

What does this have to do with funding Response Leadership and a Readiness to Act? A great deal, in fact.

Lack of funding was a major obstacle when I asked Response Leaders what some of the challenges were.

The direct and indirect cost comparison in the product security case study is a big reason why.

If you're planning an event that costs $100,000 but that's designed (and there are objectives to support it) to bring in $300,000, then it's easier to quantify and qualify where the money's going and from where it's coming.

Fundraising is not my strength, but I'm confident that there are harder things to do than raising $100,000 from investors with a clear path for them to triple their money.

On the other hand, planning for uncertainty is much more complicated:

- An unknown event
- Happening at an unknown time
- At an unknown place
- Impacting an unknown number of people
- Requiring the activation of an unknown number of responders
- Lasting for an unknown amount of time
- Costing an unknown amount of money to restore

Lots of unknowns. That list is the poster child for something that's neither quantifiable or qualifiable.

If the organization has performed adequate contingency planning, then a list of potential problems and a funding solution may already be in place.

However, for the organizations that have adopted a "that won't happen here" philosophy to event planning, a tougher road lies ahead.

Funding Sources

Funding comes from two (2) principles sources:

1. **Internal** – dues, donations, budgets, cost savings, revenue, etc.
2. **External** – investors, lenders, donations, sponsors, grants, etc.

Particularly with external funding, a substantive plan must be in place to qualify for the funding. That plan should include such things as grant or loan applications, investment proformas, etc.

Grant authorities, banks, investors and other outside funding sources need all of those facts, figures and value propositions spelled out for them in a real way. When they feel good about where the money is going and what they will see happen in return, they'll be able to make an informed choice and therefore be more engaged in the process.

Finding Grants

The federal government offers this helpful hub of grant providers and resources: https://www.grants.gov/

Writing Grants

Philanthropic Research, Inc. which collects data on thousands of nonprofits each year offers these tips from successful grant writers:

1. Request guidelines, annual reports, and other pertinent information from the foundation before sending a grant proposal. You may be able to download most of this information from the organization's Web site.

2. Unless your organization is a national one, try to stay local when looking for funding sources, particularly for operating or program costs. National foundations are more likely to fund capital expenses of programs that replicate nationally.

3. Do you know the trustees? If the foundation is local, run the names of the trustees and foundation staff by your board. They often run in the same circles, and one phone call can help put your grant proposal on the top of the pile.

4. Work with your program staff to be sure your information is up to date and relevant. The staff can also provide you with anecdotes and client testimonies that you might not otherwise have.

5. Although it is often the nature of the beast, try not to wait until the last minute to prepare your grants. Do not use Express Mail to send your application. Using Express Mail can signal to the grantmaker that your organization is a poor steward of funds.

6. Don't send a lot of "fluff" attachments. Many grantmakers will specify what to send. Don't send more than they request.

7. When you receive a grant award, be sure to send progress reports, whether requested or not. Keep in touch with your funding sources.

8. Some foundations can be very picky. They have their reasons. If they specify page length, page margins, typeface, etc., be sure to follow the specifications.

9. Before mailing out your grant proposal, call the foundation to be sure you have current contact information.

10. Many groups use a "Common Grant Application," developed by groups of grantmakers to ensure that all applicants provide the same information. Be sure to check individual foundation guidelines to see if they use this tool.

Carefully review the grant requirements as they can differ widely for each provider. Following their rules are obviously necessary to receive external funds.

One of the mistakes I've seen response organizations make is to dramatize the request instead of being more logical and pragmatic.

"We deserve the funding support because we're the ones that make sure the lights stay on."

"We don't want what happened to the Acme Corporation to happen here, so we deserve the funding support."

"We are the best chance to find Little Timmy when he goes missing, so we deserve the funding support."

Those requests come across as entitled and are usually and summarily ignored.

Regardless of where you're seeking funds, earning the necessary financial support can be a lot like earning the necessary executive support.

1.   Start by being clear about the 'what' and the 'why.'
2.   Support it with accurate forecasts of future needs.
3.   Include realistic training, education and equipment requirements.
4.   Demonstrate the features but highlight the benefits.

I remember one instance of clever wordsmithing, where a group failed to receive funding for the acquisition, training, and equipping for a "Search Dog" because dogs 'had to be fed,' 'they might bite someone,' etc. The group went back later with the same funding proposal but with a new description. Instead of calling it a search dog, they promoted a "Biological Detection Device," and they received funding right away.

I wish it were that easy, but I know it's not.

Features v. Benefits

Features get noticed, but benefits get funded.

Example:

Feature	Benefit
"This car goes 0-60 in 5 seconds."	*"This car will enrich and invigorate your life!"*
"This coffee has 95mg of caffeine."	*"This coffee will enrich and invigorate your life!"*

Feature	Benefit
"This plan will train 30 people in advanced widget tying skills!"	*"This plan will enable us to survive and thrive after a disruption!"*

What is the value proposition of this product or service?

Would you rather have useless stats to remember or be enriched and invigorated?

Would you rather be able to survive and thrive or know that 30 people can tie knots, etc.?

The answer is clear, we all want to experience the benefit more than hear about the feature. And the people and committees that can provide financial support are no different.

Even with that, some people are hard-wired to see every expense as a line item. In the response business, however, that can prove to be perilous.

Example:

- "John" is a Response Leader in the field who just had the difficult job of removing a body from a collapse.
- In his search for a moment of calm, John opens the cooler for a bottle of cold water.
- The cooler is empty, so he requests more water through his chain of command.
- That request makes its way to the funding authority who sees that a case of water costs, say $5.00.
- The request is delayed or denied because that funding authority thinks that the water hose back at the base is suitable for hydration.
- John goes without a bottle of cold water and the needed respite.
- The funding authority saves $5.00.

Or did they?

John in our story is not a line item. He's the internal customer.

And the 'feature' of a water hose a quarter mile away does little to address his needed 'benefit' of immediate hydration at the time when he most needs support.

When we view and promote other Response Leaders as internal customers, it becomes easier to make positive and impactful decisions.

When (not if) the funding authority is still stuck on whether to fund a feature or support a benefit, one the questions I challenge others to consider is this:

"What would you do if it were YOUR beloved family member who's impacted by this event?"

If they have funding authority and they're stuck on whether to approve the purchase of better emergency escape lighting versus new furniture for the lobby that question will usually get them unstuck.

Equipping

Your D.U.F.F.E.L. B.A.G.:

1. Developing
2. Unifying
3. Forecasting
4. Funding
5. **Equipping**
6. Learning
7. Boosting
8. Assessing
9. Getting Ready to Act

"Equip the man, not man the equipment." ~ Troy Brooks

In February of 2003, the US Space Shuttle exploded on re-entry and left a field of debris all over East Texas.

To help put the response to this event in perspective, it was the first national event after the terror attacks of September 2001. Between 2001 and 2003, officials spent millions of dollars in homeland security grant money, new responders hired, and trailer-loads of equipment acquired by hundreds of 'alphabet soup agencies.' Alphabet soup agencies earn that reference because they stereotypically show up wearing windbreakers with alpha characters on them like FBI, DEA, ATF, EPA, NASA, etc.).

Patriotism in the United States was also very high at that time, so when the bell went off for these agencies to respond, they showed up in droves eager to put their new tools and their new people to work.

Except their eagerness was replaced with bewilderment when they opened the trailers to discover that all of their new whiz-bang equipment still wrapped in plastic, never opened. Oh, and since they never opened the boxes, nobody knew how to use any of it either.

Most reading this might say that at least they had new equipment and that, like being burdened with lottery winnings, it's a good problem to have.

Yes, a good problem to have perhaps but irresponsible and even worse, quite common.

Having the equipment and not knowing how best to use it is worse than not having the equipment at all.

Unfortunately, there's a peculiar reality about funding equipment purchases. It's extremely common that the funding for the equipment purchase does not accompany any funding to train people to use it.

This gap between the equipment cost and the cost for the training to use the equipment is particularly common at the end of a budget cycle. I'm occasionally contacted by both private-sector companies and public-sector agencies at the end of their fiscal year asking what equipment I can sell them.

They tell me that they have money left over in their budget and need to spend it by such and such date. I ask if that purchase includes training and the answer is always "no."

I suppose it's because new widgets are easy to account for, to replace at the end of their duty cycle and don't have many ancillary costs. Training a human to be proficient at operating that widget is not nearly as streamlined from an accounting perspective.

And the result for many is: *tools get funded, and training does not.*

That's why I'm not surprised when a well-funded agency shows up to a disaster or large exercise with fancy tools that none of their folks are proficient at using.

Nonetheless, the previous steps in The Response Leadership Sequence™ should validate the need and the benefit of having the right equipment for the job at hand.

Once the equipment is acquired, it needs a home.

NOTE: Yes, it's an assumption that the requested equipment is acquired. I'm well aware that sometimes even our best efforts prevent us from acquiring the tools we need.

Organizational policies will usually determine how and where response-related equipment is stored and maintained.

A cautionary note for organizations that have not addressed this yet: Be sure to store the equipment in a place where it's quickly accessible to the Response Leaders that are trained to use it.

Sometimes, equipment policies put things under lock and key, barcoded and put in a storage room or off-site behind some other barrier. When the 'brown stuff hits the oscillating device' and that equipment is needed, it needs to be accessible.

The last friction point about equipment is that when you spend big money on it, some people may bristle at the idea of its use in a training environment. These detractors may believe that their operators will automatically be proficient using the new, unopened equipment.

This disconnect is another area where a Response Leader will make their case to procure a duplicate item for training purposes while the other item stays right-and-ready for a real event.

This challenge is also an opportunity for the Response Leader to circle back to the previously outlined unifying objectives to remind any detractors why using the equipment is needed.

Adequate tools and training are what breathes life into our Readiness to Act.

Learning

Your D.U.F.F.E.L. B.A.G.:

1. Developing
2. Unifying
3. Forecasting
4. Funding
5. Equipping
6. **Learning**
7. Boosting
8. Assessing
9. Getting Ready to Act

"People don't want to buy a quarter-inch drill; they want a quarter-inch hole." – Theodore Levitt

---

After 20+ years and over 12,000+ adult students, I've learned that people don't want to be instructed or trained, they want to learn and in many cases, transform into a better version of themselves.

Specifically, they want to learn the exact tools and techniques needed to accomplish their goals. If their goals tie to the organization's goals, great. But if not, the tie goes to the learner.

The reality of learning is that it's always occurring. Because reinforcement is always happening.

- Perhaps we're actively learning how to tie a specialized rescue knot ...
- Perhaps we're mentally learning how to lead differently than our last boss ...
- Perhaps we're passively learning how to earn an extra biscotti from the coffee shop barista ...
- Perhaps we're inadvertently learning the wrong way to assemble a widget ...

What we learn is optional, being in a state of constant learning is not.

"We don't rise to the level of our expectations; we fall to the level of our training." ~ Archilochus

---

Learning in the context of building quality Response Leaders is pretty straightforward.

By having a clear direction and ample support, learning should be laser-focused on the supporting the objectives.

If an objective includes everyone knowing how to redirect the network communications to a warm site or recovery site, then subsequent training should target what exactly people need to know to do that.

If that is the objective and we send our staff to learn how to weave baskets underwater instead, then we rightfully run the risk of alienating the support we worked hard to earn to get this far.

Similarly, and much more common, is when the objective requires a capability of a level 8 or above out of 10 and we only train them to a level 2.

Example:

I noted this regularly among disaster responders that want to – or are expected to – know how to "safely operate in and around collapsed buildings." The class they're sent to only covers 25% of what they need to know to "safely work in and around collapsed buildings" and then their training stops.

Sadly, those are the responders who willingly or unwillingly expose themselves and their team to the incredible risk of injury or death. Hardly what the objective had in mind when originally agreed to.

If we're going to pack a D.U.F.F.E.L. B.A.G. full of goodies, adequate knowledge and skill should take up most of the room.

A reminder of the knowledge and skill that's in your D.U.F.F.E.L. B.A.G.:

1. Developing
2. Unifying
3. Forecasting
4. Funding
5. Equipping
6. Learning
7. Boosting
8. Assessing
9. Getting Ready to Act

Ethically (professionally) and morally (personally) the requirement to perform the right skills at the right time in the right way is one of many characteristics of a world-class Response Leader.

And skill development has no shortcuts.

Skill-building

Before

Skill building starts with the instructor and course developer.

The topic to be learned must meet a couple of standards before the student participant ever steps into the classroom (online or in-person):

1. Relevant to what the student needs to learn to improve.
2. Delivered by competent and experienced instructional staff.
3. Identifies the skills that need evaluation.
4. Describes the type of delivery: classroom, online, or blended.
5. Provides available certifications to be earned.
6. Predictable length and location of the delivery.

Most students have other options besides attending our class, even if they need the skill. It's important that we stay focused on this commitment they are making toward our class so that we can remain committed to them and their learning.

During

Assuming the instructional staff is comprised of competent instructors, they will describe the learning outcomes expected from the class as well as other course expectations.

Communicate reasonable work (learning) and rest periods so that the students know when they are provided breaks to make calls, use the restroom, etc. As a general rule, adults should not sit for more than 50 minutes at a time and no more than 20 minutes is ideal.

The sequence of learning a new skill should follow a successful sequence, such as:

1. Demonstrate the skill at full speed.
2. Deconstruct and explain the skill.
3. Encourage questions.
4. Demonstrate the skill while narrating the key steps.
5. Encourage questions.
6. Demonstrate the skill at full speed again.
7. Encourage questions.
8. Explain the steps the students will take.
9. Encourage questions.
10. Coach the students through each step, reinforcing them as they go.

The above is a sample outline and certainly doesn't indicate the only way to introduce and teach a skill.

The Boy Scouts of America (BSA), use the "EDGE" method to teach young scouts new skills:

1. **E**xplain the skill.
2. **D**emonstrate the skill.
3. **G**uide the skill.
4. **E**nable the skill.

When teaching adults, I sometimes start with the student performing the skill and building off of that performance and many other variations. The value to the student should drive what approach you take.

Detailed information about providing different kinds of feedback is included separately in this program.

Pre-Tests and Post-Tests

Some training includes a pre-test and a post-test to measure knowledge. What they're really measuring is the competency of the instructor. Pre- and post- tests do little for the student besides increase their testing anxiety which is why I don't use them unless my client requires it.

After

1. *Tell them what you're going to tell them.*
2. *Tell them.*
3. *Tell them what you told them.*

It's usually appropriate to summarize the skill, to address any unanswered questions and to reconcile any injuries or equipment loss/damage.

After the course delivery is also a good time to reinforce any earlier statements about what the skill does and does not allow them to do.

Example:

The 4-hour Swiftwater Awareness course and associated certificate do not entitle you to participate in active water rescues from a boat.

Small Unit Leadership

The primary focus of this program is to develop and improve the skills needed by Response Leaders at ALL levels of an event.

For the most part, the skills are universal and useful for single person events all the way up to those involving thousands of people.

Somewhere in the middle is the leadership within the leadership: smaller groups of Response Leaders that work within larger groups of Response Leaders.

This dynamic is partly mindset, partly education and like everything else a Response Leader does, it requires practice to be deliberate and precise before it's needed.

Specialty Tactics

At the small-unit level, there must be a highly functioning system of cooperation, flexibility and specialty tactics consisting of things like:

1. Response leaders may or may not be the highest-ranking person in the group.
2. Multiple job skills may be required to replace having a team full of specialists.
3. More of some types of equipment or less of another type may be needed to keep the team mobile and flexible.
4. Capacity to communicate within and outside the unit. Perhaps there are people in the unit that have a different communications protocol or perhaps a different, redundant plan is needed altogether. (Communications is detailed separately in this program)

Contingency plans may be different (and more consequential) than those identified at the organizational level.

Just like the larger readiness initiative, small units also need to boost their knowledge and training by effectively exercises their skills.

Without exercising their skills in a simulated environment, they cannot be expected to perform those same skills in a real-world event.

Boosting

Your D.U.F.F.E.L. B.A.G.:

1. Developing
2. Unifying
3. Forecasting
4. Funding
5. Equipping
6. Learning
7. **Boosting**
8. Assessing
9. Getting Ready to Act

"To train the mind, you must exercise the patience and determination it takes to shape the steel." ~ Dalai Lama

---

Rockets sit on the launch pad until they are boosted with fuel to enable propulsion. Once the rocket leaves the launch pad and leaves the troposphere, the training and the effort that went into the rocket launch is validated.

To validate our response plans, they also must be boosted by leaving the safety of the training ground.

Event simulations can challenge the knowledge and skills gained in training and can provide valuable discovery for future improvement.

I've evaluated hundreds of event simulations through the years and believe strongly that these exercises are the most fertile ground for refining one's mastery of their skill.

There are several types of exercise scenarios for nearly any occasion. In the United States, the Homeland Security Exercise and Evaluation Program (HSEEP) guides the development and implement exercise programs. They identify seven types of exercises:

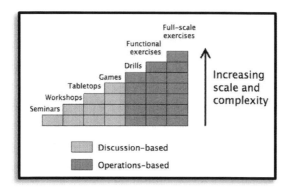

Discussion based simulations – everything from a:

- 1-on-1 "what if" discussion up to
- A classroom that's full of Response Leaders having a discussion shepherded by a trained facilitator.

Operational-based simulations – everything from:

- A simulated event with everyone sitting around the same table (frequently called a Table Top Exercise or TTX) up to:
- A simulated event that's in a simulated environment, with the full array of responders, equipment, and facilitated scenarios

Each type of simulation is intended to boost the results of the team's training.

NOTE: One of the most common friction points in a simulation is the tendency for unskilled evaluators to inject 'gotchas' into the simulation as a way to embarrass the participant and to elevate their self-important position as a perceived all-knowing overlord or both. Don't do that.

Again, the objective of these scenarios should be to strengthen the participant's capabilities through facilitated outcomes.

Facilitators

I have a well-documented position, or soapbox, regarding the use of only qualified coaches, mentors, evaluators, and facilitators. Scenarios can be stressful for a participant who wants to perform well. These vulnerable moments can also be golden opportunities for an experienced facilitator to instill confidence, courage, and trust too.

- Good facilitators can bring out the very best from the participants, who in turn will be more engaged and full of effort.
- Poor facilitators can poison a participant's experience and cause them to disengage.

Just because someone is experienced or senior in the organization does not mean he or she is qualified for the role of an exercise facilitator.

So where do we find good facilitators?

One of the most underutilized opportunities that these scenarios provide is the chance to do more coalition building.

To affirm the strength of your coalition, members can and absolutely should support your larger scenarios, in some capacity:

Examples:

- A representative from the local police or fire department evaluates the response scenario of a volunteer response organization.
- C-Suite executives being provided a VIP guided tour through the scenario to see what they are supporting. (I once put an executive who was wearing a suit into a concrete rubble pile during an exercise ... he loved it and funded the organization soon after!)
- Other (even competing) groups that perform similar functions that reciprocate their evaluation of your scenario for your evaluation of theirs.

At the conclusion of every exercise, a comprehensive debriefing should occur that captures what went well and what needs improvement.

Those findings should be objective, documented and forward-looking (blaming is for amateurs).

I discuss a more detailed process of analyzing the exercise separately.

Before it's all said and done, Response Leaders safely demobilize the people and things used in the exercise so that they restore their Readiness to Act.

Assessing

Your D.U.F.F.E.L. B.A.G.:

1. Developing
2. Unifying
3. Forecasting
4. Funding
5. Equipping
6. Learning
7. Boosting
8. ***Assessing***
9. Getting Ready to Act

"No man is capable of self-improvement if he sees no other model but himself." ~ *Conrado I. Generoso*

A notable hallmark of all high-performing organizations, along with the people that serve inside of them is their unbridled commitment to improving continuously.

Sadly though, there's no shortage of lip service given to this concept.

Organizations tell their staff that they want to be better, smart and faster all the time, right? And then when it's time to invest in staff improvement in the form of education, support and the removal of obstacles many of these organizations fall flat.

> *It's not enough to just have a plan ...*
> *It's not enough to just equip yourself ...*
> *It's not enough to just train ...*
> *It's not even enough to boost all of that by exercising ...*

World-Class Response Leaders also squeeze every ounce of improvement from every opportunity. And everything is an opportunity.

As I've mentioned, there are few better opportunities to boost performance than by a well-implemented exercise program. Inherent in such a program should be the continuous comparing and contrasting of plans and training with the agreed to objectives.

- When they are aligned, keep doing those things.
- When they are not aligned, align them, then keep doing those new, aligned things.

Example:

Two findings from last week's scenario:

1. Cyber folks and Business Continuity folks worked well together – Team building objective met, keep doing this!
2. Scenario ran late, so some participants had to drive home later after working 14 hours – Participant safety objective NOT met – refine the approach and try again.

Always remember: lots of people invested lots of time and money into the organization to get this far, so it's critical that they start to see how that investment is paying off.

Few things obliterate support faster than wasting the organization's time, money and effort to develop an event response plan that has no hope of actually addressing the challenge.

There is a more formal process to filter these findings called the After-Action Report and Improvement Plan (AAR/IP). We'll discuss this process in greater detail separately in this program.

Getting Ready to Act

Your D.U.F.F.E.L. B.A.G.:

1. Developing
2. Unifying
3. Forecasting
4. Funding
5. Equipping
6. Learning
7. Boosting
8. Assessing
9. ***Getting Ready to Act***

"In playing ball, or in life, a person occasionally gets the opportunity to do something great. When that time comes, only two things matter: Being prepared to seize the moment and having the courage to take your best swing." ~ Hank Aaron

---

When I first started training my dog for search & rescue one of my early mentors cautioned me about training and talking but not actually showing or demonstrating any real results.

As in many industries, I suppose, dog handlers tend to boast a lot about their accomplishments. This misplaced arrogance is especially pervasive with volunteers who came from organizations without a solid grasp or commitment to professional ethics, etc.

One of my mentors frequently reminded me that:

"When the tailgate drops, the B.S. stops."

And boy-o-boy has that been proven true repeatedly in my career so far.

The point is that this program, this field of study, this entire mindset of preparing is all meaningless without the Readiness to Act.

Later in my career, I was fortunate enough to be able to serve my country at many large national natural disasters like Hurricane Katrina, Ike and others. Out all of the souls that we helped take from a bad place to a better place, many of them have stayed with me, mentally.

Each disaster seemed to have its share of people of every age, gender, color, neighborhood, etc. that:

1.   had a fair amount of preparedness supplies but
2.   didn't use them to improve their condition when it mattered most.

Example:

The guy was standing on his 2nd-floor balcony with his wife and kids. His entire 1st floor was under water. He chose to not accept a boat ride to dry land because he 'had all the preparedness supplies he needed.' His wife, who told me that those 'supplies' were all on the fully submerged 1st floor, was less than enthused. He might have had the supplies and a plan, but he lacked the Readiness to Act on them. And he and his young family were in a bad way as a result.

Being Ready to Act is not just preparedness. Readiness to Act consists of a D.U.F.F.E.L. BAG full of capable plans, skilled people, and relevant experiences:

1.   **Developing**
2.   **Unifying**
3.   **Forecasting**
4.   **Funding**
5.   **Equipping**
6.   **Learning**
7.   **Boosting**
8.   **Assessing**
9.   **Getting Ready to Act**

And the Response Leader Mindset provides the spark that puts it all into motion.

Response Leadership Case Studies:

Let's look at some case studies of Response Leadership in action:

Case Study #1: Paynesville Sports Association

Paynesville Sports Association is a non-profit organization that provides seasonal sports leagues to the Paynesville community. They receive funding through player registrations, sponsorships, concession sales and spare change found underneath the bleachers. In their largest annual fundraiser, they host a tournament once per year that brings in hundreds of teams competing at multiple venues. As a result of this tournament, the Paynesville Sports Association meets or exceeds its annual income and growth expectations.

Their success factors are:

1. Selecting qualified leadership to be responsible for the tournament
2. Establishing and communicating clear objectives that address the leader's intent
3. Delegating and empowering core, functional roles to staff members
4. Selecting and implementing strategies that support the objectives
5. Identifying and removing obstacles that impede accomplishing the objectives
6. Supporting each functional role player with the resources they need to be successful
7. Utilizing relevant tactics that maximize results

Case Study #2: Baron's Computer Service

Baron's Computer Service is a small business operating out of 8 area locations:

- Four stand-alone retail locations,
- Two mall kiosks,
- One small office warehouse and

- One headquarters location (the founder's home office), which also houses the company's network server.

The company has grown by at least 20% each year, enjoys a loyal customer base, has low employee turnover and virtually no inventory shrinkage from theft or loss.

Their success factors are:

1. Selecting qualified leadership to be responsible for the business
2. Establishing and communicating clear objectives that address the leader's intent
3. Delegating and empowering core, functional roles to staff members
4. Selecting and implementing strategies that support the objectives
5. Identifying and removing obstacles that impede accomplishing the objectives
6. Supporting each functional role player with the resources they need to be successful
7. Utilizing relevant tactics that maximize results

Case Study #3: Evans Family Vacation

The Evans family consists of a mom, dad, four kids (ages 8-16), a dog and an elderly grandparent. They decide to go away for summer vacation to Disney World. They set a budget, arrange for travel and lodging, and pack their bags. During the vacation, they meet everyone's expectations, they minimize their personal and financial risk, and their memories were happy and healthy.

Their success factors are:

1. Selecting qualified leadership (mom and dad) to be responsible for the strategy decisions
2. Establishing and communicating clear objectives that address the leader's intent (fun, risk management, adventure, etc.)
3. Delegating and empowering core, functional roles to staff members (kids pick order of the attractions they will attend)

4. Selecting and implementing strategies that support the objectives (staying near park to reduce travel time and rental car expense, booking a large suite to provide personal space for all, etc.)

5. Identifying and removing obstacles that impede accomplishing the objectives (having activities that accommodate the limitations of small kids and elderly grandparent, etc.)

6. Supporting each functional role player with the resources they need to be successful (creating growth opportunities for each family member to in turn help grow the family's success, etc.)

7. Utilizing relevant tactics that maximize results (all-inclusive park passes, dispensing individual allowances for the kids, etc.)

You might notice - especially if you've participated in a successful family vacation before - that many of these success factors are what you already do or have already considered. That's great! This program will help improve your current level of planning and strengthen your understanding of the fundamental principles that need integrating into every plan, not just one you use for vacations, etc.

Case Study #4: Saloma Community Hospital

The Saloma Community Hospital operates 500 beds, a Level 2 trauma center and an eight-bed ICU. They have a staff of 200 consisting of patient care personnel, administrative, facilities (including engineering and security), a part-time staff of 20 and a roster of 40 regular volunteers.

In April, their facility was impacted by an EF3 tornado. They lost power, and part of their patient care area suffered some degree of wind and water damage to approximately 43 rooms. 2 of their on-duty staff members are unaccounted for, and 7 of them have reported minor injuries.

They were able to recover their facility and staff, restore patient care, reduce ongoing risk to their staff, patients, visitors, and vendors in record time. They completed all of the work at a minimal expense.

Their success factors are:

1. Selecting qualified leadership to be responsible for operating the hospital during good times and during a crisis
2. Establishing and communicating clear objectives that address the leader's intent, for planned and unplanned events
3. Delegating and empowering core, functional roles to staff members
4. Selecting and implementing strategies that support the objectives
5. Identifying and removing obstacles that impede accomplishing the objectives
6. Supporting each functional role player with the resources they need to be successful
7. Utilizing relevant tactics that maximize results

Three case studies, three different sets of objectives, all with the same success factors.

How did they do it? Can your organization be more successful during planned and unplanned events? Read on ...

The Response Leadership Sequence™ - Part 2 (The Trigger)

Every planned and unplanned event follows a sequence. And either the sequence controls us, or we control the sequence!

Therefore, the more organized and predictable we manage that sequence, the more efficiently our event will flow and the greater the chance we can prevent unforeseen challenges.

The Response Leadership Sequence™ provides a planning process that Response Leaders can use for events that are big or small, planned or unplanned.

The Trigger

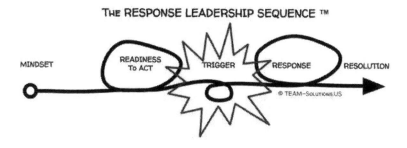

The trigger is the action that initiates the actual response.

- For planned events, it's the previously mentioned Mission intent/statement where the Response Leader addresses the *what* and the *why*.
- For unplanned events (like a disruption of some kind), the initial action is the disruption followed immediately by the leader communicating the *what* and the *why*.

In either case, this initial trigger is what propels us through the Response Leadership Sequence™.

These over-arching WHAT and WHY statements provide the framework of our initial objectives.

And those refined, initial objectives are what bring life to our event planning.

So, the next two primary steps in the sequence are to:

1. **Confirm/Assess the current situation**
2. **Validate/Refine the current objectives**

Thankfully, many events find a resolution quickly, easily, and with minimal intervention even when a leader is prepared to manage it through completion.

If an unplanned trigger occurs (like the ubiquitous spilled cup of coffee), most folks will be suitably equipped to swiftly clean the spill up and then move on with their day. No escalation of people or resources would be needed.

The circular nature of the trigger represents the initial reactions needed to determine if future actions would be needed to manage such an escalation.

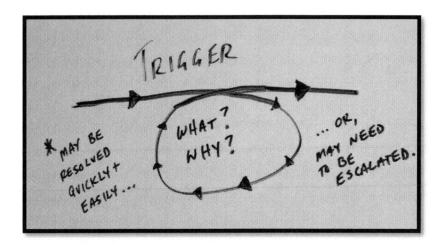

In a small event these reactions may be taken by one or two people, but in larger events, more effort is needed to accomplish the initial 'size-up.'

If the event is large or is expected to become large, the sooner that you start collaborating and coordinating with other responding Response Leaders the better the outcome will be.

<u>For example:</u>

> In 2012, there was a mass shooting at a movie theatre in Aurora, Colorado. The police department responded because it was a shooting, the fire department responded because it was a mass casualty event and Emergency Medical Services (EMS) responded because people were injured.

> The fire department established a command post and immediately instructed all EMS resources to report to a nearby parking lot. At the same

time, the police department had already started transporting victims to local hospitals in their police cars.

All three agencies that had the statutory responsibility to respond (Police, Fire, and EMS) were all doing their own thing and not communicating effectively or collaboratively with each other. To their credit, the police tried to join the fire department command post but were told to wait.

It's evident that having a representative from each response organization working together is better for the customer (the shooting victims) than working apart, yet stories like above are common.

Later in this text, we'll discuss in greater detail the formation of Unified Command. When operating with a unified command, each agency has representatives in the same command post, and they make decisions jointly.

One reason is that, initially, leaders are commonly and even expectedly consumed with reacting to the trigger rather than leading through it.

Therefore, for responders to elevate their leadership beyond merely reacting to the crisis, they must construct an initial incident management plan consisting of five (5) pillars.

Pillars of Command

"If I had six hours to chop down a tree, I'd spend the first hour sharpening the ax." ~ Abraham Lincoln

---

Generally speaking, until the following activities have occurred, the Response Leader is more focused on responding rather than on leading.

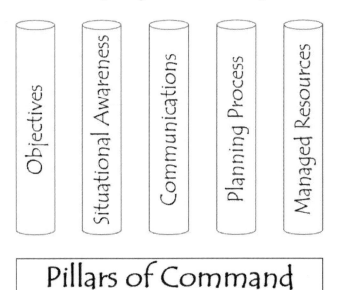

In no particular order, the Pillars of Command are:

1. **Situational awareness achieved**
2. **Objectives identified**
3. **Communication plan implemented**
4. **Planning process underway**
5. **Functional resources managed**

(Credit to the Los Angeles Fire Department for providing these 'Pillars of Command')

Reaction Phase v. Managed Phase

"It's not what happens to you, but how you react to it that matters." ~ Epictetus

---

It bears repeating that until establishing these pillars, we are still reacting to the crisis, conditions may still be chaotic, and our blind spots may still be sizable.

To a degree, the crisis is still controlling us.

Not until we achieve initial situation awareness, identify some initial objectives, put a communication plan in place, implement a planning process, and establish a procedure to manage resources are we starting to manage the crisis.

However rudimentary those pillars are initially, that improved condition marks the beginning of the managed phase.

Afterwards, the managed phase will exist until we resolve the crisis.

Below is what the phases look like within The Response Leadership Sequence ™:

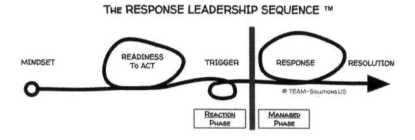

THE RESPONSE LEADERSHIP SEQUENCE ™

EXAMPLE: Spilled Coffee

Now to illustrate the point using the simple example of a spilled cup of coffee:

1. Initial trigger: cup of coffee spilled on the counter
2. REACTION Phase:
   a. Mission: to clean it up (WHAT) ... in order to maintain a clean countertop (WHY) (our initial, unrefined objective)
   b. Current Situation: Coffee is still on the counter and is dripping onto the floor
   c. Current Objective to clean up coffee: still valid!

If the coffee was STILL flowing, and the floor ruined as a result, or there were other issues, just reacting would not be enough.

We would need to build a managed response, led by a capable Response Leader.

Since it would take more than a few minutes to resolve this expanded event, the plan for how to solve it must expand also.

Those plans consist of the "here and now" which addresses the current problem and the "hereafter" which addresses the remaining, future problems.

The hereafter plans are developed and implemented over subsequent work cycles called operational periods.

Operational Periods

"Work expands to fill the time available for its completion." ~
Cyril Northcote Parkinson (Parkinson's Theory)

How do you eat an elephant? One bite at a time. And that bite needs to be small enough to chew and swallow, right?

<u>Example:</u>

The initial search and rescue mission to Hurricane Katrina took over a month before it shifted to a search and recovery mission. We worked all day tirelessly, then did it again all day the next day and so on.

Each of those days was a separate operational period. Sometimes the plan was a duplicate of the previous day and sometimes our operations had a different focus.

As the name implies, an operational period refers to the length of time that resources will be active in the field conducting assigned operations.

Planning for those operational periods is one (1) operational period behind.

Here's an operational period example borrowed from an unplanned event:

1. Tornado (trigger event) happens on Monday evening. The Response Leadership Sequence™ begins (Op Period #0)
2. Monday evening you arrive to lead the response and create objectives.
3. Monday evening you determine that it will take several days to achieve the objectives.
4. Monday evening you and your team start planning for Tuesday's operations (Op Period #1).
5. Tuesday morning begins Op Period #1 and planning for Wednesday (Op Period #2).

6. Wednesday morning begins Op Period #2 and planning for Thursday (Op Period #3).

That process continues until there are no more objectives to achieve.

Planned events, like a 4th of July parade, would follow a similar pattern (in simple terms):

1. Decide to have a parade (trigger event). January 1st. The Response Leadership Sequence™ begins.
2. January 15th – July 1st the planning process is in effect (Op Period #1)
3. July 2nd – 3rd final preparations take place (Op Period #2)
4. July 4th – parade operation (Op Period #3)
5. July 5th – parade demobilization (Op Period #4)

Each operational period includes the process of identifying resource requirements, requesting additional resources, and developing an Incident Action Plan (IAP).

Separate lessons will address this managed phase in much greater detail.

For now, we can start ramping up the next phase by looking more critically at our initial objectives.

Even though the response to a spilled cup of coffee is simple and intuitive, let's SMARTen up the objectives needed to resolve this unplanned event.

Other Response Planning Models

As I mentioned at the onset, if there were a better way to improve, simplify and unify crisis response, I'd be sharing that information instead.

As of now, though, The Response Leadership Sequence™ represents the most comprehensive model to meet those objectives.

Nonetheless, there are other planning models found in material related to business continuity, project management, and incident management, to name a few.

Example:

In 1970 southern California was besieged by wildfires. The 'incident-level operational coordination,' a/k/a Response Leadership didn't go very well, so they created a system called FIRESCOPE, which stands for "**FI**refighting **RES**ources of **C**alifornia **O**rganized for **P**otential **E**mergencies."

Their contributions to Response Leadership include the original iterations of the Incident Command System (ICS), originally called the "Field Command Operating System," and a response planning sequence in the shape of a wheel.

As response organizations outside of California started embracing the benefits of ICS, it was evident that ICS applied to more than just fires. With a shift toward an 'All-Hazards' approach, the US Coast Guard modified the FIRESCOPE "wheel" into the "Planning P," which many agencies still use. It provides a guide for the initial response period (the 'leg' of the "P") and the first operational period of the "P" (the 'top').

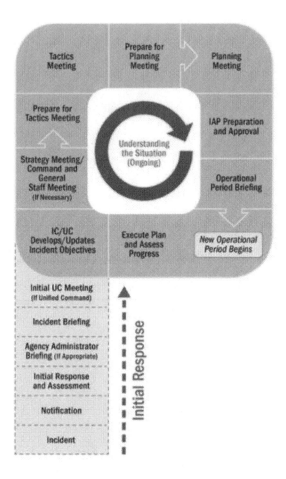

Each relevant step of the "Planning P" is represented in The Response Leadership Sequence™.

Later in this material, I prove a comprehensive timeline of the meetings/briefings, attendees, and forms that are consistent with both the "Planning P" and The Response Leadership Sequence™.

S.M.A.R.T. Objectives

"The successful people are those who have objective interests which absorb them, thus making them an object of interest to others." ~ George Odiorne

---

It starts with objectives.

Objectives that are S.M.A.R.T. are more likely to be achieved than objectives that are not S.M.A.R.T.

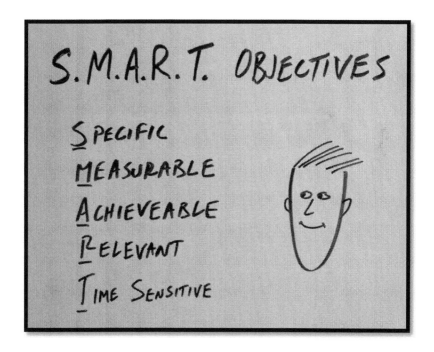

S.M.A.R.T. objectives are:

Specific
Measurable
Achievable
Relevant / Realistic
Time Sensitive

For example:

Status: You're hungry

Not S.M.A.R.T. Objective: Eat

S.M.A.R.T. Objective: Go now to the Kroger grocery store at 123 Main Street, purchase a tray of sushi-to-go, an apple and a 16-ounce bottle of water.

For example:

Specific - yes, it identifies specific grocery store and specific food to obtain
Measurable - yes, it identifies amount of food to purchase
Achievable - yes, the store is within walking distance
Relevant / Realistic - yes, it addresses the desire to eat
Time Sensitive - yes, it requires going to the store now

For the spilled cup of coffee our S.M.A.R.T. objectives may look like this:

A. Immediately protect oneself by reducing the risk of being burned by the hot coffee.
B. Clean up the spilled coffee on the counter and floor.
C. Restore supplies and refill the coffee cup with fresh coffee.

Could they be even SMARTer? Sure. The SMARTer they are, the easier they'll be to understand and achieve. However, there can be as much art as science in developing S.M.A.R.T. objectives in a timely fashion.

Warning: At some point, the effort to SMARTen them up may steal from the time it takes actually to work to achieve the objectives! Think seriously about them but avoid over thinking!

Again, since most people reading this have spilled a drink on the counter, the objectives needed to respond have become intuitive and subconscious already.

232

In fact, it's helpful to know that the most routine events are resolved immediately after the trigger, with no escalation. And that's great! This program addresses the events that exceed the ability to resolve them instantaneously.

So, by illustrating and validating them here, we can begin to understand how our current, mostly effortless, objective-based thinking can be improved and expanded to address more complex events.

Other planning actions useful for more complex events - like contingency planning and information management - will be discussed in a separate lesson.

Examples of S.M.A.R.T. Objectives

Below are some sample objectives used by Response Leaders with varying degrees of 'SMARTs' that may be appropriate and adapted for most responses.

Note: The below objectives are not 'one-size-fits-all,' so carefully consider their interpretation before mandating their use.

1. Provide for the safety of responders and the public/citizens for the duration of the incident
2. Provide for responder safety through the adherence to agency policies and SOP's (Standard Operating Procedures) during incident operations
3. Evaluate safety concerns for incident personnel and public thru utilization of risk management principles
4. Ensure proper PPE (Personal Protective Equipment) is worn and follow appropriate safety procedures at all times
5. Evacuate all residents between _____ and _____ Streets by _____ hours
6. Facilitate orderly evacuation of the affected area/scene/endangered persons
7. Continue to evaluate the effectiveness of the evacuation boundary
8. Construct sandbag diversion away from _____ by _____ hours
9. Monitor activities and respond to maintain peace, order and life safety
10. Maintain a functional emergency response system
11. Maintain/Provide/Establish normal public safety operations/services
12. Provide for immediate & on-going Life, Health & Safety needs
13. Return all public facilities used for the response to at least minimal operational conditions by _____ hours
14. Maintain facility isolation

15. Access & document damages of the impacted areas
16. Complete a damage survey within 12/24/ or _____ hour
17. Complete preparations for all aspects of _____ operations
18. Continue reconnaissance at _____ by _____ hours
19. Create appropriate documentation to support response (Search & Rescue) efforts
20. Continue on-site assessment of critical infrastructure
21. Complete an "Areas of Risk" Assessment/Size Up
22. Continue to coordinate operations between agencies
23. Manage a coordinated response effort
24. Provide and control support to the incident/event command
25. Keep Costs Commensurate with Values at Risk
26. Utilize best practices relative to cost and time management
27. Ensure a positive work environment for all personnel
28. Maintain high visibility throughout the community
29. Support the physical needs of staff and rescue workers
30. Evaluate requests for assistance as received from external entities
31. Protect Private Property, Improvements, and other Commercial Endeavors
32. Maximize /Continue/Monitor protection of environmentally sensitive areas
33. Minimize economic impact of the affected area/community
34. Provide resource support for the community
35. Continue volunteer management efforts
36. Provide ''just in time'' training for responders (searchers) that arrive to assist
37. Meet the basic needs of affected residents
38. Communicate with Unified Command to ensure compliance with _____
39. Keep stakeholders, responders and public informed of response activities
40. Establish a program committee that includes wide participation from your company.
41. Assess your current preparedness program.
42. Reach out to public emergency services and regulators. Ask for input.
43. Conduct a risk assessment to identify threat and hazard scenarios and significant loss potential.
44. Conduct a business impact analysis to identify the operational and financial impacts of interruption or disruption of your business.
45. Identify opportunities for hazard prevention and risk mitigation.
46. Protect the safety of your employees by developing evacuation, sheltering and lockdown plans. Conduct employee training and drills.

47. Install an emergency generator to power the data center during a power outage.
48. Develop plans to equip and configure Plant B as a backup for Plant A.
49. Upgrade the protection of the facility by installing a fire sprinkler system.
50. Phase out the use of highly toxic or flammable chemicals.
51. Conducting a full-scale exercise of the emergency management program involving public emergency services.
52. Shifting some or all operations to a location that is less susceptible to natural hazards such as earthquakes, hurricanes or flooding.
53. Building a culture of preparedness in the workplace and encourage employees to have a plan at home.

Special thanks to members of the Texas Forest Service (TFS) for contributing to this list of sample objectives.

How many objectives are needed? The rule of thumb is to have enough objectives to address the challenge at hand. Initial objectives need to address incident priorities like life safety, incident stabilization, and property preservation. I've seen anywhere from three objectives that address those priorities to as many as fifteen.

As The Response Leadership Sequence™ progresses, there is an opportunity to add, subtract, or modify your objectives.

For complex incidents when the list of objectives expands beyond four or five objectives, requesting an All-Hazards Incident Management Team (AHIMT) is often a good choice to manage all or part of the incident. Conversely, when the objectives contract to three or four remaining objectives, that may indicate that the AHIMT is no longer needed.

Expanded detail on Incident Management Teams is provided later in this program.

Let's revisit the Pillars needed to move out of the Reaction Phase and into the Managed Phase.

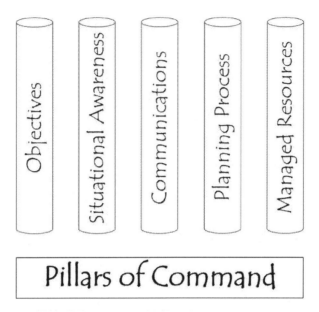

In no particular order, once the Response Leader achieves some initial situational awareness and identifies some initial objectives, there are still three additional pillars that need addressing.

Remember a 100% solution is not needed, just the foundational framework of each component to enable future response success.

- **Situational Awareness** – "knowing, understanding, and anticipating" as previously discussed in a separate section.
- **Communications** – Having the means to communicate throughout the organization. This topic is covered in-depth separately in this material.
- **Planning Process** – The backbone of a successful response isn't the presence of a plan, it's the commitment to a planning process. This process will be covered extensively -depth in the next section.
- **Managed Resources** – Similarly, managing resources effectively will be the focus of a separate section in this material.

Whether one person or one-hundred people have responded to the crisis, the initial leadership team must point them all toward establishing the pillars above.

I provide some of the meetings/briefings, attendees, and forms that help during complex incidents in a separate section.

Response Leadership (Reacting & Managing)

As the event plan continues to expand, so does the need for more Response Leaders to help support the objectives.

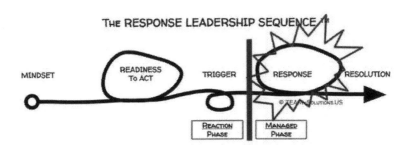

For instance, if someone calls 911 to report a missing person, the first police officer that arrives typically is 'all things to all people,' i.e., they perform ALL necessary functions ... until they delegate it.

Important: This initial Response Leader must have both the responsibility and authority to coordinate resources to meet the objective.

In an unplanned emergency, this statutory responsibility typically falls to the police, fire, and emergency medical services.

For planned events, this may be a policy maker, CEO, school principal or any other leader with influence, authority and responsibility for managing an event.

After a quick analysis of the situation and of the initial objectives, a common result is:

1. The event will become unmanageable without a sensible plan
2. The organization must expand its available resources to achieve the objectives

For example:

- One spilled coffee = one-person resource

238

- EF4 tornado through neighborhood = many, many resources are needed

5 Leadership Functions

"The function of leadership is to produce more leaders, not more followers." ~ Ralph Nader

---

To expand our organization, we must first identify the five (5) leadership functions that are present during every event.

For example, when coffee spills, these functional areas may look like this:

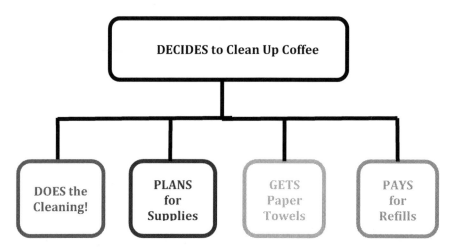

The use of common language is critical in our efforts to reduce confusion and to promote understanding.

So that we're using the same description, here are the functional titles we'll be using and the primary focus of their activity:

> **Event Coordination / Incident Command function** - *DECIDES stuff*
> **Planning function** - *PLANS for stuff*
> **Logistical function** - *GETS stuff*
> **Operational function** - *DOES stuff*

Administrative/Finance function - *PAYS for stuff*

When we apply these functional roles to our spilled cup of coffee example:

- You spill the coffee (**event is triggered**)
- You decide to clean it up and to get more coffee (**Event Coordination function**)
- You identify the need for paper towels, sponge, trash can, and more coffee (**Planning function**)
- You gather paper towels and cleaning supplies from the supply cabinet (**Logistical function**)
- You clean up the coffee, throw away the trash, and make more coffee (**Operational function**)
- You order replacement supplies and coffee (**Administrative/Finance function**)

How many people are needed to solve the spilled coffee event? Just one, then it's done. No need to complicate the clean-up with extra people, right?

However, even though only one person manages this simple job, the above five (5) critical functions will all occur to some degree.

Now let's look at these functions from a hierarchical perspective.

Organizational Chart - Simple

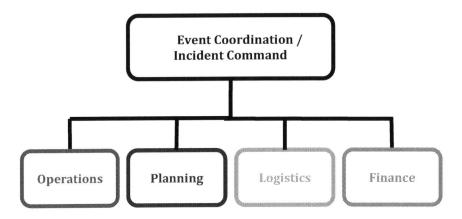

<u>A couple of critical notes:</u>

- This model is the same one the emergency services use, where the use of the chain of command (line of authority within the organization) and unity of command (everyone only has one boss) is critical.
- During planned events, consistency and predictability are also important, but expect more collaboration and flexibility since everyone is expected to be a contributing Response Leader.

As our event expands (or contracts), these essential functions may also expand (and contract).

It should be clear how roles expand and contract based on what's needed so let's revisit the spilled cup of coffee. Except we'll add a little more complexity and a little more realistic staffing.

In this instance, the coffee spills on a piece of electronic equipment in addition to the desk, some sensitive work documents and the carpet.

As we consider the functions that play an active role, they may break down like this:

1. Event Coordinator and Operations are the only functions activated.

2. The Event Coordinator (you) also cleans up the coffee, papers and some of the carpet (Operations)
3. Someone from IT is needed to assist with the electronics and someone from the janitorial staff is needed to assist with deep cleaning the carpet. (also, Operations)

Still functional based, still ready to expand or contract but only activating the roles that are required, when they're required.

Here's how it may look like in hierarchal form, even though there would be no need actually to create this for such a simple response:

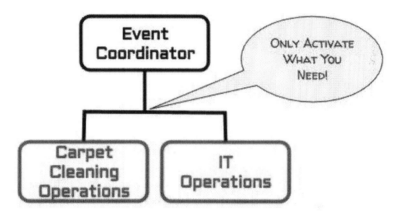

As long as everyone is embracing the responsibility that comes with his or her role, accomplish the work at hand by no more and no less than the job requires.

A Unified Command

Unified command is a rare but extremely valuable strategy to coordinate large events.

Here's an example:

A bad guy shoots multiple diners inside the local restaurant. He also starts a grease fire in the kitchen before running out of the back door.

The primary emergency response resources that have a role to play are:

Police – to investigate the crime
Fire – to put out the fire
EMS – to treat the injured

Each entity has a statutory responsibility to respond. In other words, it's their job, and they have to go. Bill the Landscaper, on the other hand, does not have to go because it's not his required job.

Once on scene, each entity will be peering at the chaos through their specific filter, understandably.

If the police took command, the response might not address the subtleties of an expanding grease fire or the intricacies of a treating a gunshot victim.

And the EMS and Fire representatives would face similar challenges if they were responsible for addressing the unique strategies required for a competent police response.

Unified Command addresses this by consolidating each entity in a unified command role. Each commander retains their authority, but they all collaborate with each other to develop single, unified objectives instead of three separate command posts operating under three separate sets of objectives. One of the Unified Commanders usually agrees to serve as the spokesperson, but they each have an equal contribution about what is said.

Diplomacy rules obviously, but when the right people are in place, Unified Command can dramatically increase the effectiveness of a response.

A note for my military readers: the military uses the term 'unity of command' to explain that one commander is responsible for each stated objective. That reference is separate and apart from the Unified Command construct presented above.

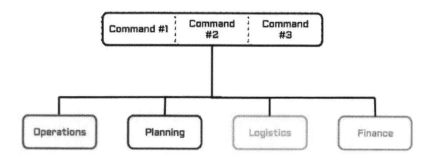

Delegating Authority

Identifying the rightful owner of a disaster is surprisingly clear-cut.

Ownership lives where the disaster originated.

<u>Example:</u>

- If Rick spills his coffee on your desk, you own the disaster.
- If an EF3 tornado wipes out your office, you own the disaster.
- If the Town of Creekview floods, the Town of Creekview owns the disaster.

Of course, other parties may have a responsibility too. (*"Come on, Rick! Go get some paper towels!"*) but the ultimate owner is who is usually 'left holding the bag.'

Now let's say the event was to expand because the problem has exceeded the ability for the owner to address it adequately:

- The janitor is needed to help clean up the coffee stain on the carpet.
- The landlord is needed to send contractors to help rebuild.
- The County of Riverbank is needed to help arrange for Search & Rescue support.

Most of this support is the result of the **size** of the event changing, i.e., it's grown into a bigger problem than we can handle alone.

However, sometimes escalation must occur because of the **scope** of the event changes, i.e., it's grown more complicated than we can handle alone.

When the complexity of the event intensifies, the owner of the disaster may not have the skills or availability to handle it.

In this case, enter a Delegation of Authority.

Typically, a Delegation of Authority essentially gives the delegate the green light to do two (2) things on behalf of the 'owner':

1. Spend the owner's money
2. Direct the owner's resources

Example:

- Giving Rick $20 and telling him to clean up and repair any damage from the spilled coffee.
- Hiring a contractor to oversee the restoration of your office building.
- Appointing an Incident Management Team (IMT) to lead the flood response.

A Delegation of Authority is best done in writing and co-signed by the authority and by the delegate. While there's not a standard for what to include in one, here are some considerations:

- Any restrictions.
- Reporting requirements.
- Political implications.
- Any priorities.
- Communication and disclosure expectations.
- Criteria to transfer the event back to the original owner.

With a Delegation of Authority, the owner of the disaster never relinquishes ultimate responsibility. They simply transfer the care and custody of that responsibility to a more appropriate entity.

To some, 'delegating' and 'authority' are two words that suggest the need for an armada of lawyers to approve the process first. Since a crisis seldom has the time for a legal convention, a "Letter of Expectation" is used in place of a Delegation of Authority, which essentially does the same thing just without the ominous title.

Organizational Chart - Intermediate

When the event organization needs further expansion, it won't grow beyond the primary five functional positions. However, each function will grow internally.

This description addresses "who" is involved in an expanded event. "How" they manage it is discussed in greater detail later.

Here are some examples of the organization may grow:

- The Event Coordinator/Incident Commander function may expand to include a person overseeing the overall safety of the event, a liaison to policy makers, etc.
- The Operations function may expand by having geographical (i.e., "North Branch") or functional branches (i.e., "Site Management Branch") that help manage the operations.
- The Planning function may expand by having people assist with resource planning, situational awareness, etc.
- The Logistics function may expand by including a unit that feeds responders, a unit that manages an event facility, etc.
- The Finance and Administration function may expand to include a unit that procures needed items, a unit that tracks costs, etc.

Here's an expanded perspective:

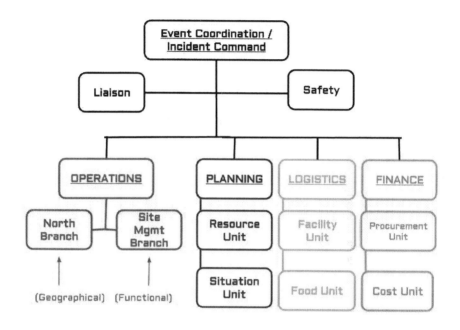

Command and General Staff

The top of each functional section in Operations, Planning, Logistics, Finance/Administration comprise what is called the General Staff.

- The Event Coordinator / Incident Commander and their other direct reports (Liaison, Safety, etc.) comprise the Command Staff.
- So, everyone that is a chief of a functional section and above is known as the Command and General Staff.
- This designation is meaningful, especially during significant events.
- The Command and General Staff manage the organization.

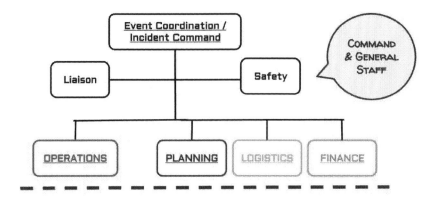

The functional sections manage the event.

Example:

Beyond just a box on an organizational chart, if the Event Coordinator leaves their box and tries to direct the meal delivery to the volunteers, then the event and its participants will ultimately suffer.

If this were to occur:

1. The Event Coordinator is no longer, you know, coordinating the event organization.
2. The Food Unit Leader has lost their trust in the Event Coordinator since they were the one initially delegated the task.
3. The Unity of Command (everyone only has one boss) breaks since the Event Coordinator has stepped beyond the authority of the Logistics Section Chief (who is the one boss to whom the Food Unit Leader should answer).

Unity of Command is an ICS construct that ensures that directions are not contradicted. The idea is that everyone only has one boss, i.e., only one person giving them instructions and in turn, they are their subordinate's only boss.

Remember, once a task is delegated and empowered, our job is to:

1. **Promote the Mission**
2. **Remove Obstacles**

3.   Provide Support

Stepping into someone else's 'box' for any other reason is a no-no.

Also, each "box" represents at least one person. As that one person's ability is exceeded to manage that function, then that function will need to expand also.

Example:

If there are 100 people to be fed at three different event sites, then the Food Unit may need to expand to involve more people to meet the objective. After meeting the meal-related responsibilities, the Food Unit may scale back (or disband entirely) based on the current and planned needs.

The organizational structure is scalable, to expand or contract functional positions as the event requirements dictate. Scalability is one of the core features of ICS.

Span of Control

"What counts is not necessarily the size of the dog in the fight but the size of the fight in the dog." ~ Dwight D. Eisenhower

---

- How many people are needed to manage a group of subordinates?
- How much is enough and how many is too many?

It's common for someone to want to tackle all of the tasks themselves. Very common.

While it's possible to succeed with that strategy, it's unlikely. There are far too many specialized tasks requiring focus and skill, therefore, trying to remain the only decision-maker doesn't represent a superior practice.

On the other hand, it's also popular to have only one layer of supervision to give everyone the feeling that 'everyone is in charge.' This flat organizational model adds to the challenges of accountability, communication, and duplication of effort, so it's also not an ideal strategy for managing a successful event.

Where, How and Why Span of Control is Important

"No man can command more than five distinct bodies in the same theater of war." ~ Napoleon I (1815)

The oft-repeated dictate on how many subordinates one supervisor can have has been around a long, long time.

If you've taken a FEMA course on how to manage an emergency response, you've heard this chant ad nauseam about the span of control:

"Span of Control is 3 to 7, with 5 being optimal." ~FEMA

That means that every student, from every class, from every derivative class, and then their disciples all spout the same math. That, in turn, leads crisis managers near and far to force that definition into every personnel configuration they perform or direct. Ugh.

The problem though is that this Napoleonic, one size fits all approach is simply wrong. Stacking a crew with more - or less - people than the task needs is poor resource management. And poor resource management can lead to costly mistakes. And who among us can afford a costly mistake?

Let's break it down.

For starters, a span of control is a tool to help managers improve their management. It is not a tool to help subordinates perform and complete a task better.

If the task that needs managing is complex and requires active managerial input, then a smaller ratio of supervisor-to-subordinate (a span of control) is needed.

Example:

You're managing a team of people to team-carry a live panther while navigating an obstacle course that's on fire. On the edge of a cliff. Blindfolded. The supervisor will be busy directing traffic, and the subordinates must be hyper dialed-in. The team size will likely be as small as can reasonably perform the task. Synchronicity reigns and any more than a small handful of subordinates would stretch the supervisor's ability to supervise. *And the risk to the Team **increases**.*

However, if the task that needs managing is not very complex and requires very little managerial input, then a larger ratio of supervisor-to-subordinate (a span of control) is needed.

Example:

You're managing a team of able-bodied people to slowly skip from one end of a 1-acre field of allergy-free tulips to the other end of the field. Each of them skipping at their own pace. The supervisor will not be very busy and the subordinates can self-direct their actions. The number of people on the tulip skipping team can likely be as large as the field will accommodate. Even a large group will not unduly tax the supervisor's ability to supervise. *And the risk to the Team will **NOT increase**.*

So, no matter how much time, money and people you have available to throw at a task, remember that establishing and maintaining proper span of control is more about risk management than it is about math.

It should be clear by now that there's a level of risk in everything we do, right?

Lastly, to boil this down to the teaching point I use in my classes:

- *The complexity of your task and your level of risk tolerance determines your span of control.*
- *If that ends up as an optimal team of 5, then so be it.*

In 2017, FEMA finally softened their guidance, but I expect it to be years (or generations) before its understood.

A few other special-use considerations of this functional based system:

- Two positions, one person.
- Early in an event, it is common for multiple roles to be executed by just one person.
- As the event expands, however, the roles should be separated and the additional roles delegated to additional people.

Example:

Tom is executing the role of Event Coordinator (under Command), Operations Section Chief (under Operations) and Situation Unit Leader (Plans/Situation Unit). The organization chart may look like this:

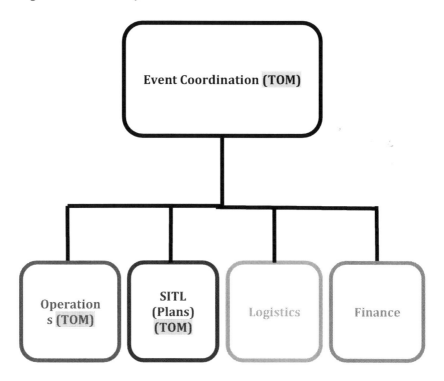

As previously mentioned not every position has to be filled!

> Example #1 - It's uncommon for a full Administrative and Finance Section to be activated and filled at the command post level. Those functions are often handled at the agency level (it is their money after all!)

> Example #2 – Remember the earlier example of "Tom" being the Situation Unit Leader, a position within the Planning Section? Even when requiring the function of the Situation Unit for the event, a Planning Section Chief may not need to be activated simply to supervise them. It may be just as appropriate - and resource-wise - to activate the Situation Unit as the only representative of the Planning Section.

> If or when conditions change, more personnel can be activated and added later.

Most positions can have helpers!

For instance, Command and General Staff positions can assign a Deputy. The important thing to remember about Deputies is that a Deputy has all of the capability and all of the authority as the Chief in that Section. This configuration becomes especially useful when the Chief is at a meeting or is off-duty (managing their work/rest cycle!), and someone needs to be able to make a Chief-level decision.

Similarly, within the sections, as responsibilities and tasks grow, Assistants can be assigned to virtually any position to spread out not only the workload but also the span of control.

Here is a table of some of the more common Units that are available for activation for each section:

COMMAND	OPERATIONS	PLANNING	LOGISTICS	FINANCE/ADMIN
Safety Officer	Branches	Resources Unit	Support Branch:	Procurement Unit
Liaison Officer	Divisions	Situation Unit	Supply Unit	Time Unit
Public Information Officer	Groups	Documentation Unit	Facilities Unit	Cost Unit
	Units	Demobilization Unit	Ground Support Unit	Compensation/Claims Unit

COMMAND	OPERATIONS	PLANNING	LOGISTICS	FINANCE/ADMIN
	Strike Team/Task Force	Technical Specialists (Weather, etc.)	Service Branch:	
			Communications Unit	
			Medical Unit	
			Food Unit	

Because of the critical functions they perform, let's take a closer look at the Situation Unit working under Planning.

The Situation Unit

Even though it's every Response Leader's job to share and promote situational awareness, it's the Situation Unit that brings it all to life.

When a Response Leader at virtually any level of the response needs information, they will receive it from the Situation Unit.

Organizationally they are positioned under the Planning Section and are led by a Situation Unit Leader or SITL.

Some of their major responsibilities consist of:

1. Collecting and analyzing event or incident information.
2. Distributing event or incident information through briefings, displays, and other distribution.

Their real value comes in actively obtaining event or incident related information.

Since the Situation Unit Leader is likely sitting at a computer terminal updating a common, major event log, they are aptly assisted by data collectors frequently called Forward Observers, or FOBS.

FOBS are valuable wherever there is activity occurring. When properly positioned, they're able to provide almost real-time updates to the Situation Unit, and in turn, the Response Leaders that rely on current information to make decisions.

1. In a command post or Emergency Operations Center (EOC), they proactively visit each section to notate what is on display and ask for verbal or written updates from command post staff.
2. In the field, FOBS are often able to shadow Response Leaders working in the field. Since they see and hear first-hand information that way, the data is less likely to be wrong when shared by the Situation Unit.

NOTE: FOBS working in the field have special requirements. Since they are usually operating alone, their risk is significantly higher. Also, they must be known and clearly identified by field responders, so they're not mistaken for an intruder.

These "FOB's" may also funnel their findings to the Situation Unit's designate - called "Information & Intelligence" - who will usually filter the data before it is posted publicly to other event staff.

The Situation Unit utilizes other forms of data collection, too. For example:

*   Field Observers (FOBS)
*   Crime Analysts including Fusion Centers
*   Dispatchers
*   Human Intelligence
*   Media (social and traditional)
*   Other Response Leaders in other operations centers

Even though the Situation Unit reports to the Planning Section, they do not have to position themselves inside the Incident Command Post. In reality, they will likely be more effective if they are in a separate area where they can stay hyper-focused on their various forms of data collection with minimal distractions.

Response Leadership & The Command / General Staff

"Lead me, follow me, or get out of my way." ~ General George S. Patton

---

I'll emphasize here that even though we are talking about mostly a hierarchical system, it does not mean that we reserve leadership for only those at the top.

The entire premise of Response Leadership is that everyone is expected to be a leader by doing what leaders do: support, advocate, remove obstacles, etc.

One of the ways to ensure that the leadership mission stays at the forefront of our decision-making is to participate in relevant and regular Command and General Staff meetings.

The Incident Command System provides us the titles of the Command and General Staff, and their meaning is universal enough that they are relevant to virtually any responder.

Especially during a fast-paced event, these 'huddles' can be extremely valuable to detect early warning signs of trouble.

On the other hand, avoid meetings that don't have a purpose at all costs!

Escalation

"You can never solve a problem on the level on which it was created." ~ Albert Einstein

---

Initially, handle all events at their lowest possible level.

The best case is when the event can be resolved quickly and easily after the trigger. Here we're talking about when the event is complex and is growing even more complex.

So far, we've addressed how events start small and then expand as the need requires. Such as activating the Planning Section or adding a Facilities Unit in Logistics, etc.

Similarly, if an event starts to go from being in control to being out-of-control, escalating the entire response is reasonable.

Example:

Think of a structured classroom environment where there's an 8 to 1 student-to-instructor ratio. If at the last minute 4 more students enroll making a total of 12, then another instructor should be added to maintain the integrity of that ratio.

NOTE: As an aside, if a course delivery exceeded the student-to-instructor ratio some agencies will invalidate a student's certificate of completion.

Event response is similar. If accomplishing the objectives is not attainable with the resources on hand, then the savvy Response Leader will incorporate more or different resources to keep ahead of the event's escalation.

- Sometimes the escalation requires adding resources below them to work on the response.
- Sometimes the escalation requires requesting coordination above them to support the response.

When the Incident Command Post requests coordination and support from outside the immediate event area, here are some buttons that may get pushed:

- **Dispatch Center**: it's essentially calling 911, but from internal customers instead of from the public.
- **Emergency Operations Center (EOC)**: they are usually one level removed from the event command post, and they help coordinate extra support and resources needed from outside the event perimeter, like evacuation shelters, communications networks, resources from a far away jurisdiction, etc.
- **Department Operations Center (DOC)**: these are where the Response Leaders are within a specific organization or entity, such as a dedicated cyber response team inside a hospital. They may also send folks to be represented in an EOC to support the larger incident.
- **Multiagency Coordination (MAC) Group**: MACs are like the elementary, intermediate and high school superintendents at the school district. During the district-wide carnival, these representatives from each level can authorize and coordinate resources from their respective campuses to support the district-wide effort. They can do this without being at or near the event itself.
- **Area Command**: Area Commands are an event coordination structure that manages multiple incidents that each have command posts. For example, think of 4 non-contiguous homes that are on fire in a neighbor of 200 homes. At each home, there's a different incident commander that's coordinating that home's fire event from their command post. At the entrance to the neighborhood is a 5th command post dedicated to supporting and coordinating the overall activities at each fire. That coordinating command post is where the Area Command works.
- **Incident Management Teams (IMT's)**: IMT's are on-demand Response Leaders. They typically will bring a complete Command and General Staff as well as some specialty positions. They are also 'typed,' so a Type I is a large group of qualified Response Leaders for a national level event (major disaster) and a Type IV is a smaller sized group of local Response Leaders.
- **Disaster Declaration**: Disaster Declarations are legal distinctions, made by governments and supported by documentation, where a local agency raises the flag and says they're in over their heads. When Smallville is the epicenter of a disaster, and they're unable to handle it (including

the inability to afford the cost of recovering from it) they seek support from the county or next, higher-level jurisdiction. When approved, the county can use their funds to assist Smallville in their costs of response and recovery. When the county's abilities near their capacity, they seek a Disaster Declaration from their regional or state emergency managers. And in turn, the state can seek a Disaster Declaration from the federal government.

Sometimes, when the event escalates in size and scope, it also requires more time to solve the problem.

During these types of escalations, additional operational periods are appropriate, as discussed previously.

I'll share the strategies and tactics used to plan for future operational periods separately.

Recruitment and Coalition Building

"It is possible for a leader to go out and recruit people unlike himself, but those are not the people he will naturally attract." ~ John C. Maxwell

---

When the organization starts to expand, if there's not a deep pool of responders to fill the need, the event begins to flex beyond its available capacity.

Therefore, the process of building that roster of qualified contributors should start long before the event is triggered.

Developing, unifying, forecasting, funding, educating and learning are addressed in-depth earlier in this program.

Resource Leadership

"One cannot manage too many affairs: like pumpkins in the water, one pops up while you try to hold down the other." ~ *Chinese Proverb*

A crisis, especially an escalating crisis, can quickly be overrun with all kinds of people and all kinds of things. While that may seem optimal on the surface, consider these examples:

- After the Sandy Hook school shooting in 2012, a separate building needed renting, and people had to be assigned to receive, inventory and otherwise manage the onslaught of unsolicited gifts.
- After the World Trade Center terrorist attacks in 2001, public statements to stop sending doggie booties were necessary as they were arriving by the truckload (disaster dogs don't wear booties unless they are protecting an injury).
- After the Space Shuttle Columbia explosion over Texas in 2003, responders had to be pulled from their assignments to assist in the management of thousands of untrained volunteers who showed up to help uninvited.

Even when invited and needed, the sheer mass of some incidents can produce sizable resource management challenges.

- Hurricane Ike in 2008 is the largest search and rescue operation in Texas history, requiring the management of thousands of trained responders.

Managing the complexity of these invited and uninvited resources requires a plan.

First, here are the primary resources categories:

People - personnel requested and utilized by the event organization
Things - Equipment and supplies utilized by the event organization
Places - facilities utilized by the event organization

Planning Strategies for People, Things, and Places

There are two primary strategies to staff the organization for the event adequately.

1. Matching up resources to what we already have
2. Identifying and requesting resources we don't have

The second strategy, identifying and requesting resources we don't have, will be thoroughly discussed in a separate section.

Initially, however, the current organization needs analyzing.

Successful Resource Planning using a Litmus Test

If an organizational structure already exists, compare those objectives to the configuration of the current organization. This comparison is sometimes called a "Litmus Test" by my colleagues who served in the LAFD. This comparison exercise is primarily an indicator of future success or failure in meeting the objectives.

The "Litmus Test" is a method to determine if the commander's intent (objectives) are being accomplished with the current field resources. This illustrates whether the system is under-built or if the system is overbuilt and resources are being wasted.

For instance, if an objective is to keep the event area clean and the trash emptied, then an analysis must occur that ensures that there are adequate janitorial resources assigned to the operation.

If not, then those resources must be ordered or requested in order to accomplish the objective.

Using the simple example of responding to a spilled cup of coffee, let's look at some sample objectives.

Objectives:

A.   Clean up spilled coffee
B.   Replace broken mug
C.   Refill new mug with coffee
D.   Drink fresh mug of coffee

Remember, we use letters instead of numbers to avoid the implication that there is a priority at this point.

To further the example, here is a look at how the current Operations Section may appear.

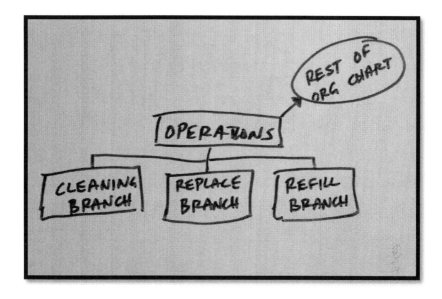

To confirm that resources are available to be assigned to each objective, link each objective to each functional branch.

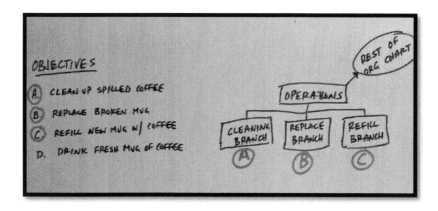

Like this:

A. Clean up spilled coffee → Cleaning Branch
B. Replace broken mug → Replace Branch
C. Refill new mug with coffee → Refill Branch
D. Drink a fresh mug of coffee → ?????

This Litmus Test isolates the issue that one of the objectives ('Drink a fresh mug of coffee') does not have resources assigned to accomplish the objective.

After identifying this issue, the Operations Section and the Command Staff can discuss the creation of an additional branch ('Drinking Branch') under Operations that can be assigned the extra objective ('Drink a fresh mug of coffee').

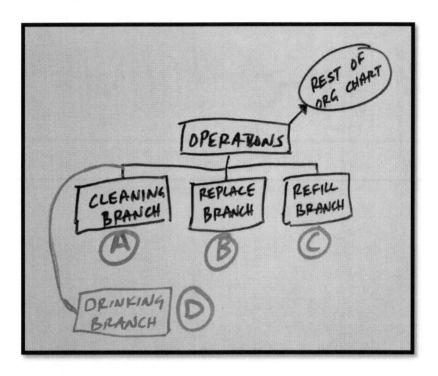

Using this Litmus Test process whenever objectives are created or updated helps the Response Leader confidently maintain the necessary balance of having enough resources to accomplish the required objectives.

Resource Ordering Principles

Three (3) basic principles should be evaluated when considering additional resources:

1. **Planning**
2. **Organizing**
3. **Supervising**

Planning

Additional planning and analysis should occur when:

- Resources to fill an organizational structure don't currently exist, or
- If the event will extend beyond the availability of the current resources

Example:

After conducting a Litmus Test, event planners realize that an overnight security team is needed to fulfill the objective of providing 24 hours of protection.

Organizing

Once the requested resources arrive at the Staging Area and are available for service, organize them so that they best meet the objectives.

Example:

The Acme Security Company sent a van carrying ten additional security officers. Arrange them to include a mobile supervisor in the van with an assistant and the remaining eight divided into 2-person foot assignments.

Supervising

Proper supervision helps to maintain a sensible span of control, reinforce clear lines of authority and maximize effective communication.

Like any Response Leader, a supervisor is there to help their subordinates accomplish the objectives by providing support and removing obstacles and not by exercising unnecessary control.

Planning Tactics for People, Things, and Places – Basic

Planning for resources is done in two typical ways:

1. **By Function** - defines tasks, identifies people to accomplish those tasks
2. **By Availability** - defines people available, defines (limits) tasks based on those people

"By Function" is almost always a superior choice.

Since we created S.M.A.R.T. objectives and achievable strategies, we're able to plan and manage an event without being restricted by an arbitrary number of participants.

Examples:

The furniture store's parking lot sale will be held Friday, Saturday, and Sunday during business hours. One of the objectives may be to 'promote the three-day, outdoor event to sell off excess inventory.'

The person or person's developing that objective may only see the outcome of selling off the furniture without anticipating the other resources required to accomplish the objective.

To identify and plan for the strategies and tactics needed to support the objective, people representing the following functions need to huddle.

This huddle should involve people responsible for the following functions:

- Planning function
- Operations Function
- Safety Function
- Logistics Function

Example from the parking lot sales event:

The Planning Section Chief presents the most current objectives, including:

- 'promote the three-day, outdoor event to sell off excess inventory.'

The Operations Section Chief identifies what operational resources (people and equipment) are needed to achieve each objective, including:

- Salespeople, night security, etc.

The Logistics Section Chief identifies what logistical items (supplies, equipment, facilities, etc.) are needed to support those operations, including:

- Tents to protect furniture from rain, shelter, food/water, hygiene for night security, etc.

The Safety Officer crafts a message of risk management steps to be addressed during the operations.

- Keep parking lot lights on, keep weather radio on, post signs about having security, etc.

The Planning Section Chief identifies what and how many people resources they will need to request to support the operation.

- Requests night security for each night, etc.

If the perspective of the sales manager dictated the plan, for example, they might not have identified the need for a night security guard. Bringing relevant, informed Subject Matter Experts to the planning table can pay off!

Now let's look at a more advanced method to identify, request, and manage resources.

Planning Tactics for People, Things, and Places - Advanced

Some events or incidents requires at least one additional operational period before being resolved. In that case, implement more organized resource planning.

As The Response Leadership Sequence™ moves forward, two aspects are critical:

1. **Situational Awareness**
2. **A plan for what's next**

Without them, we're clueless and unprepared, which are definitely not attributes of a capable Response Leader.

To ensure that we have optimal situational awareness and a comprehensive plan, a sensible schedule of meetings and briefings will strengthen them both.

Here's an idea of what this looks like during The Response Leadership Sequence™:

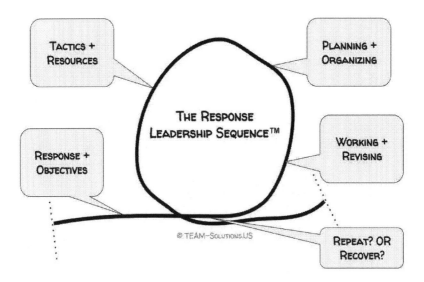

The Response Leadership Sequence™ Meetings and Briefings

"The length of a meeting increases with the square of the number of people present." ~ Shanahan's Law

---

Remember:

- Briefings are one-way communication. Hold your questions to the end.
- Meetings are two-way communication. Interact as appropriate.

The below schedule of meetings and briefings typically occurs in the listed sequence.

The intention is for them to keep everyone informed (situation awareness) and to move the response forward with a workable plan that leads to an eventual resolution.

I'll share additional details on some of the ICS forms later.

Meeting/ Briefing:	Also:	Occurs:	Attendees:	Forms:
WHAT Happened and WHY are We Here Meeting	Initial Incident/ Unified Command Meeting (IC/UC)	After the Trigger, before the full command & general staff are on scene	Current & incoming IC/UC	ICS 201 – Incident Briefing ICS 211 – Check-In List ICS 214 – Activity Log
WHAT Do We Do to Solve This Meeting	Objectives Meeting	Start of Managed Phase, after the command & general staff are on scene	IC/UC and invited command + general staff	ICS 202 – Incident Objectives

Meeting/ Briefing:	Also:	Occurs:	Attendees:	Forms:
WHO is Here to Help Us Now Meeting	General Staff Meeting	Once Managed Phase is Underway	ALL – Command Staff + chiefs/reps from Plans, Ops, Finance, Logs	ICS 203 – Org. Assignment List ICS 207 – Org. Chart ICS 208 - Safety Message
HOW and WHO Will Help Us Next Meeting	Tactical Planning Meeting	After adequate situational awareness is achieved, before requesting additional resources	Ops, Logs, Safety, Resource Unit (Plans)	ICS 215 – Operational Planning Worksheet ICS 215A – IAP Safety Analysis ICS 213 – Resource Request ICS 204 – Assignment List
Does Everyone Support This Plan Meeting	Planning Meeting	After requesting additional resources but before they arrive	ALL – Command Staff plus chiefs or reps from Plans, Ops, Finance, Logs (Plan approved by IC/UC)	Completed Incident Action Plan (IAP) incl. ICS 205 – Comm. Plan ICS 206 – Medical Plan ICS 221 - Demobilization ICS 209 – Incident Status Summary
GO Forth and Solve This Problem Briefing	Operations Period Briefing	After additional resources have arrived, before start of new operational period	ALL – Command Staff plus chiefs/reps from Plans, Ops, Finance, Logs AND Incoming Responders	Completed IAP ICS 214 – Activity Log

Meeting/ Briefing:	Also:	Occurs:	Attendees:	Forms:
WHAT Went Right and What Went Wrong Meeting?	Hot Wash	Any time an operation is complete, and there's something to learn	All participants of that operation	ICS 214 – Activity Log
WHAT Were Overall Gaps and What Overall Improvements Are Needed?	After Action Review and Improvement Plan (AAR/IP)	After the event reaches resolution	Select Command and General Staff With information gathered from each section	AAR/IP Documentation

Forms (ICS) Used for Planning People, Things and Places

"We forecast that we'll see the paperless office at the same time we see the paperless bathroom." ~ Steve Pytka

---

While detailed instruction for ICS forms and procedures is outside the scope of this material, you can download your own editable, ICS workbook with instructions from my website, TEAM-Solutions.US.

Nonetheless, outlines of some of the more common forms mentioned that a Response Leader needs to know are below. They are not all required for every response, but they all perform a purpose. By understanding their purpose, you will be able to determine best when to use them under which circumstances.

Later in this program, I explain the differences between a 'job aid' and the 'job.'

ICS 211 Incident Check-In List

The first person responding to an escalating event needs to establish an ICS 211 Incident Check-in List or equivalent.

Of course, most emergencies trigger from a call to 911 resulting in a flurry of emergency, computer-aided dispatches captured on an electronic dispatch log.

However, once The Response Leadership Sequence™ has moved from the reaction phase to the managed phase, resources will cease being dispatched and will start arriving at a Staging Area or other Incident Facility to report.

It is during this check-in process that each responder and each team should sign in on an ICS 211. The sooner this form is initiated, the easier it will be for everyone else to follow suit.

The ICS 211 also provides a helpful job aid should the need arise to evacuate an area or other reason to establish accountability.

Most organized training classes, controlled access buildings, etc. have a sign-in form procedure already so adapting one for a response should be familiar.

Akin to the Check-in List is a card system called the ICS 219 Resource Status Card, or "T-Card" because it's shaped like the letter "T." T-Cards are color-coded and list each resource, vehicle, etc. used by the incident. The Resource Unit places them on a large board with slots that visually display the status and location of each resource. T-Cards are not used much anymore but remain popular, especially for wildland firefighters who usually have extensive experience with them.

ICS 214 Activity Log

For individuals, the ICS 214 Activity Log should be filled out for each operational period and record all of the consequential activities they participated in during that period. One method to consider is capturing any of the following activities:

- Accidents
- Agreements
- Actions
- Disagreements

Many squad leaders will sometimes capture these activities onto one log for the squad since they were all together.

The ICS 214 is also later synced with sign-in records (ICS 211) and payroll records to not only pay the responder accurately but also have solid recordkeeping for seeking reimbursement from FEMA, etc. after a major incident.

An important reminder about the ICS 214 is that it's a legal record of the Incident. Whatever is in writing about your daily activity is subject to disclosure in a legal proceeding.

Be accurate, be truthful, and be mindful of what is in writing.

ICS 201 Incident (Event) Briefing

The ICS 201 documents the initial actions associated with the response and is often the only ICS form used for the first 12 hours of a response.

As mentioned previously, the data on the ICS 201 is most of what is needed when transitioning from the reaction phase to the managed phase because it documents a great deal of the situational awareness Response Leaders need early in the incident.

278

Many simple or short-in-duration events are successfully managed using just the ICS 201.

The ICS 201 is four pages long. The first two pages record major information pillars including a:

1. Map Sketch of the Incident
2. Situation Summary of the Situation
3. Current and Planned Objectives
4. Current and Planned Actions

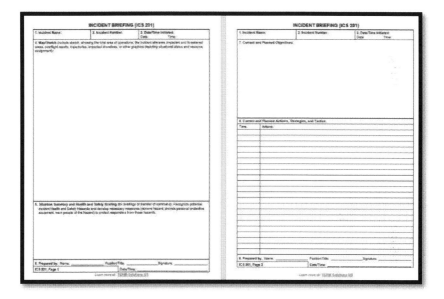

The last two pages record:

1. The current Organization Chart
2. A Summary of Activated Resources

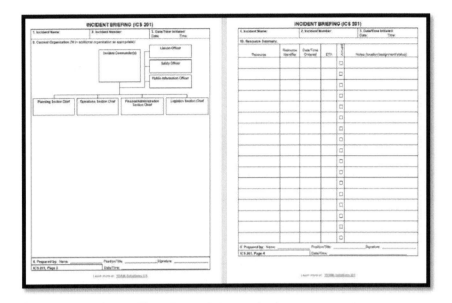

ICS 215 Operational Planning Worksheet

The ICS 215 and the following ICS 215A are as much a process as they are ICS forms. They are the work product that results from the Strategy and Tactics Meeting while planning for the next operational period.

Since resource planning is a key aspect of The Response Leadership Sequence™ expanded information about who, when, and how will follow about the Tactics Meeting.

The intent of the ICS 215 is to identify the resource requirements needed to address the objectives agreed to earlier in the planning process.

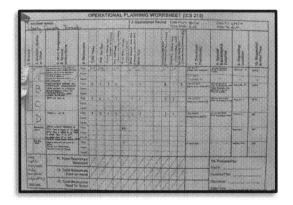

For example:

- One of the SMART Objectives is to perform a high coverage secondary search of the building on the NW corner of Walk and Don't Walk before sundown.
- Personnel from Operations, Logistics, and Plans determine that based on their experience, one Type IV Urban Search & Rescue team will be needed.
- However, since none are currently available for the next operational period, then one needs to be requested to arrive before the next period begins.

ICS 215A Incident Action Plan Safety Analysis

The ICS 215A represents the Incident Safety Officer's contribution to the ICS 215 operational planning process. The form captures specific safety considerations for those teams, with that objective, for that building.

The Resource Planning Meeting (Tactics Meeting)

The process to identify and plan for the tasks and the resources to accomplish those tasks is commonly called the Tactics Meeting.

The results of this meeting should align objectives to tasks to resources before moving to the next phase.

The aforementioned ICS 215 and the ICS 215a are two of the core products of the Tactics Meeting. Let's dig deeper into what occurs at the Tactics Meeting, who should be there, and what outcomes to expect.

After identifying the SMART Objectives, the following subject matter experts should assemble for the tactical planning meeting:

- **Operations Section Chief** – facilitates the meeting, identifies task assignments and resources needed to meet the incident objectives.
- **Resource Unit Leader (Plans)** – assigns resources to the task assignments.
- **Logistics Section Chief** – requests any additional resources needed to meet task assignments.

- **Incident Safety Officer** – performs risk assessment and recommendations for task assignments.
- **Others** – these are the Subject Matter Experts (SMEs) that the Operations Section Chief needs to augment their tactical plans, as needed.

The Tactics Meeting is a working meeting and needs to take place in a separate area, away from the hustle and bustle of the Incident Command Post. A nearby conference room is usually sufficient.

The parties listed to attend each have something different to contribute so they, or their qualified representative, are required to attend.

Note that other Response Team Leaders within the Command and General Staff are not listed; this is to limit attendance to those that need to make a proactive contribution without the distractions of non-contributors.

The steps and the existing forms that guide us through this process are:

1. **Refer to the existing WHAT and the WHO:**
   a. Incident Objectives ICS 202
   b. Incident Organization Chart ICS 207
2. **Assess and Analyze the Requirements:**
   a. Operation Planning Worksheet ICS 215
   b. Incident Action Plan Safety Analysis ICS 215A
3. **Assign the Task(s):**
   a. Assignment List ICS 204

NOTE: The Resource Unit Leader completes the ICS 204 separately from the Tactics Meeting. I list it here to connect the process to the outcome.

For example:

- The ICS 215 Operational Planning Worksheet step reveals the need for a 6-person Cyber Response Team for an identified task. However, until the resource ordering process takes place, we won't know the name or the agency that is providing that resource.
- Once the requested resource arrives in the Staging Area, the Resource Unit adds their names to the appropriate ICS 204 Assignment List. The

remainder of the data is copied and pasted from the ICS 215 and the ICS 215a.

- A copy of the relevant ICS 204 Assignment List will be eventually handed to the assigned responders before they start their task.

ICS 209 Incident Status Summary

When an event extends beyond a single operational period, documenting a summary of the incident status is helpful to plan effectively for the next operational period.

Remember, use only what is needed to get the job done.

In events that require planning beyond the initial operational period, the best practice is the creation of an Event Action Plan (EAP) for planned events or what's called an Incident Action Plan (IAP) for unplanned events.

Expanded details about EAPs and IAPs are provided in a moment.

ICS 204 Assignment List

The ICS 204 Assignment List is the one document oncoming responders are eager to read because it outlines where they're assigned and what they're assigned to do.

While the Response Leader headed to the field will gravitate toward the ICS 204, Response Leaders who are managing the incident will gravitate toward the ICS 201 since it outlines the over-arching direction of the response.

Every Branch or Group activated for the response should have their own ICS 204 filled out and a copy provided to each resource leader.

Besides detailing the work assignment – derived from the Incident Objectives and the ICS 215 – it prompts for phone and radio contact information for those in the chain of command, a safety message and a list of others assigned to the same Group or Branch.

The work assignments should be in writing and include descriptions that include:

1. Where the assignment takes place
2. What period the assignment takes place
3. What the actual assignment is (this is usually a refined version of one of the objectives)
4. What resources, from where and how many are assigned to the task
5. How the assigned resources will communicate to each other and to other event participants
6. What Risk Management considerations and special instructions apply
7. What general Situational Awareness message is applicable
8. Indication of any attachments (maps, flyers, media talking points, etc.)
9. Who approved the work assignment

A common trap is to add multiple tasks to one task assignment form to 'clear the shelves' of items to do.

The science of failing to accomplish too many things at once aka "multitasking" is pretty clear. Therefore:

Assign a task, not a 'multi task.'

Incident Action Plans (IAP) and Event Action Plans (EAP)

Just as The Response Leadership Sequence™ has a predictable flow, so does an EAP and IAP.

These document packages include all of the planning documents created to support what is supposed to happen in the NEXT operational period.

All of the relevant forms - usually in the order created - are collected and bound together for each planned operational period.

These assembled plans are the playbook for your event, and you can name them whatever works best for your organization. A complete ICS Forms Workbook is available at TEAM-Solutions.US

If you haven't already and even if you have no intention of using any of them, I recommend that you download your own ICS forms workbook. It comes with instructions for each form, and they're editable.

They are a helpful resource when you need to document something and want to use a form that already exists for that purpose.

While the majority of them are outside the scope of this program, commonly used Incident Command System (ICS) forms are:

- ICS Form 201, Incident Briefing
- ICS Form 202, Incident Objectives
- ICS Form 203, Organization Assignment List
- ICS Form 204, Assignment List
- ICS Form 205, Incident Radio Communications Plan
- ICS Form 206, Medical Plan
- ICS Form 207, Organizational Chart
- ICS Form 209, Incident Status Summary
- ICS Form 210, Status Change Card
- ICS Form 211, Check-In List
- ICS Form 213, General Message
- ICS Form 214, Unit Log
- ICS Form 215, Operational Planning Worksheet
- ICS Form 215a, Incident Action Plan Safety Analysis
- ICS Form 216, Radio Requirements Worksheet
- ICS Form 217, Radio Frequency Assignment Worksheet
- ICS Form 218, Support Vehicle Inventory
- ICS Forms 219, Resource Status Card (T-Card)
- ICS Form 220, Air Operations Summary
- ICS Form 221, Demobilization Plan
- ICS Form 308, Resource Order Form

Another document worth mentioning is essentially a function that gets put into writing.

It's called an After-Action Report, or AAR, and it's the written version of what the Response Leader(s) learned during their response.

Further discussion regarding the AAR occurs in a separate lesson.

Now vs. Later

When developing these task assignments, stay mindful of the difference between problems that are being solved now versus problems that you'll be solving later.

NOW

When an unplanned event is triggered, immediate action is required.

Example:

- A customer spills a bottle of chlorine in a closed space full of other customers.
- Directing customers and employees outside into fresh air is a NOW action and seldom would involve the use of a task assignment form.

LATER

For events that extend into future operational periods, a delay before taking any action may be appropriate.

This delay is of course also true when the people or things needed to address the problem have not arrived yet!

Example:

- Same spilled chlorine example.

- After handling the immediate priorities (life safety, and incident stabilization, remember?) then perhaps a specialized team in hazardous materials clean-up and ventilation is needed.

In this instance, the task assignment is filled out in anticipation of their arrival.

The ICS 204 Assignment List is a useful job aid that captures the critical aspects of each work assignment. ICS 204s are also prominently featured in a completed Event or Incident Action Plan.

However, other forms can perform the same purpose or can be attached to the ICS 204. So, while the components of this document are vital to advancing in The Response Leadership Sequence™, the use of this particular form is not.

Types and Kinds of People and Things

"The copier is broken again ... go get Chuck to fix it!"

"Beatrice will be running this event because that's what she always does."

Of course, in those examples, mentioning Chuck and Beatrice by name may make sense.

- They may be the most experienced.
- They may be paid to perform that function.

   Or

- We may have grown reliant on specific people instead of specific functions to complete certain tasks.

When (not if) the latter is true, consider the functional advantages of having multiple people trained and available to perform those tasks. The chief advantage being the ability to continue to perform the function when people like Chuck and people like Beatrice are not available.

"The copier is broken again ... go get someone in Engineering (function) to fix it!"

"One of our trained event coordinators will be running this event."

When availability counts, people that perform functions are more valuable than a single individual.

One of the ways to increase the chance that we ask for and receive the right resources (people and things) is to categorize them as a "kind" and a "type."

For example, categorizing a meal by "kind" and "type" looks like this:

Pizza, which is the **KIND** of meal.

And

Large, gluten-free, veggie which is the **TYPE** of meal.

In event planning, we would ask:

What **KIND** of person or thing is needed?

Example:

- I need **medics** because I have or expect to have injured people.
- I need **referees** because I have games to be officiated.

What **TYPE** of person or thing is needed?

Example:

- I need a **TYPE IV Ambulance Strike Team** to check into the Staging Area. (5 Advanced Life Support ambulances with two medics each and a supervisor)
- I need **24 Grade 8 (TYPE) Referees** due to the age groups of the competitors.

Using Types and Kinds creates a helpful gateway used by Response Leaders by which resources can be described to get the right thing, in the right amount with the right amount of training and qualifications.

Capabilities

There used to be a popular commercial on television that advertised a hotel chain. It showed a person about to perform complicated surgery on an unconscious patient. Someone else in the operating room asked this 'surgeon' - unknown to everyone else - if they had ever performed surgery on anyone before. This 'surgeon' replied:

"No, but I stayed at an XYZ Hotel last night."

The inference being that staying at their hotel gives one mastery over the task of successfully performing a complicated surgery.

If only it were that easy!

Before inviting a resource to the event, the requestor should know and be comfortable with that resource's capability level. Categorizing the resource by Type and Kind can add a lot of value, but these categories may not be common or readily available.

What kind of Hazmat team? What type of Hazmat team? Unless the Response Leader is familiar with a hazardous material response, they may not know - or care - what type or kind they need, only that their problem gets solved.

Understanding a resource's capability is less of an option though. We wouldn't want someone trained as a salesman to replace the wiring harness on our car, right?

If the resource doesn't have verifiable credentials to display, one simple question we can ask is:

"What are you capable of doing?"

While this can result in a false positive (someone exaggerating their abilities), that question can also set some critical expectations of a resource.

I'll speak about the process of capacity building separately.

Team Configuration

Understanding how to configure the arriving teams can be helpful when determining where and how to utilize them best.

Single Resources - An individual, a piece of equipment and its personnel complement, or a crew/team of individuals with an identified work supervisor that can be used on an incident.

Example: Weather Advisor, Social Media Specialist, Public Information Officer (PIO), Tow truck with the driver, etc.

Strike Teams - A set number of resources of the same kind and type that have an established minimum number of personnel, common communications, and a leader.

Example: a team of only swift water rescuers with a boat is called a Swift Water Strike Team, and a team of only gas utility workers is a Gas Utility Strike Team, etc.

Task Forces - Any combination of resources of different kinds and/or types assembled to support a specific mission or operational need.

Example: a team of utility workers that can address gas, electric, and water issues is a Public Works Task Force, and a team of disaster search & rescue responders is an Urban Search & Rescue (US&R) Team.

Remember too that these references define the type of team (Utility, US&R, etc.) but that adding the kind of team will help define and refine what they can do.

For example, a Type IV US&R team is made up of 22 people and can sustain itself for twenty-four hours whereas a Type I US&R team is made up of 72 people and can sustain itself for ten days.

For long duration or complicated events, this may make a big difference.

Resource Agreements

Sometimes the resources you need must be obtained from a galaxy far, far away and sometimes they're available locally, perhaps on a routine basis.

Similarly, if a Response Leader expects to use an outside resource on a regular basis, then an agreement can be put into effect during 'peacetime' so it will speed up the response during 'wartime.'

In either case, requesting these resources still must be authorized, and an agreement must be in place of how to use them. A common agreement for requests of these types is:

Memorandum of Understanding (MOU)

A Memorandum of Understanding (MOU) is little more than an official handshake between 2 parties.

Example: On my disaster task force, a member who is an individual resource (as opposed to being sponsored by an agency) signs an MOU that states that:

1. member agrees to respond when available and
2. task force agrees to request their services when needed.

Memorandum of Agreement (MOA)

A Memorandum of Agreement (MOA) is a binding agreement where two parties agree to a specific, joint action.

Example: On my same task force, when an agency provides their on-duty resources to support a disaster response, the member (like Kenny who is working at Fire Station 19), the fire department, and the task force execute the MOA.

The MOA will address things like compensation for back-filling Kenny's position at the station, training expectations and liability in the event of an injury.

Having a plan to handle compensation and liability need to be factored into every resource decision.

Mutual Aid Agreement

A Mutual Aid Agreement is an agreement between two agencies that address the sharing of resources.

Example: Smithville and Jonesville have a Mutual Aid Agreement in place for firefighting resources. If Smithville has a large fire in their city and they need Jonesville's assistance, they notify Jonesville, and if Jonesville has any resources available, they'll send them right away.

The Mutual Aid Agreement already spells out the subject of compensation and liability so each agency can comfortably support the other without having to hammer out those important details while their city is burning down.

Some Mutual Aid may even be automatic so that the two agencies agree to send supporting resources without even being asked.

Span of Control

Span of Control is covered in depth in the section about the *Intermediate Organizational Chart*. As a refresher, maintaining a span of control is an important measurement to ensure that supervisors are not overburdened with more subordinates than they can adequately supervise.

Span of Control: The number of subordinates for which a supervisor is responsible, usually expressed as the ratio of supervisors to individuals. ~ The National Incident Management System (NIMS)

The actual ideal number of subordinates mirrors the complexity of the task so it may be 3 for high-risk activities or 50 for low-risk activities. The most common number is 5.

Resource Tracking

"If you pay peanuts, you get monkeys." ~ Tim Harrison

The first and most important thing to know about tracking resources is that when they accept your invite to come to your crisis, you are making two very important promises:

1. You will compensate them.
2. You will cover their liability.

Example:

- Fireman Johnny arrives at his first assignment, steps out of his truck, trips, and chips a tooth.
- We, as in 'the incident,' cover his salary for being there and we facilitate the liability claim for his dental care.

Within the vast framework of forms, processes and procedures discussed, the most relevant forms to track resources at the individual and team level are:

ICS 213 Resource Request (or equivalent) – this form documents when they were requested and under what conditions (Mutual Aid, etc.)

ICS 211 – Check-In List (or equivalent) – this form documents when and what time they signed into the incident.

ICS 214 – Activity Log (or equivalent) – this form is maintained by the individual or team and shows what activities they participated in during the response.

They all are turned in at the end of each shift and become part of the official, legal, permanent documentation of the incident.

And if Fireman Johnny didn't sign-in or turn in an Activity Log? Well, he will have a very, very hard time getting reimbursed for his time and injury.

I'm aware of many examples of people and teams that did not receive remuneration because they did not supply the correct documentation.

NOTE: I realize that many Response Leaders that support an event or an incident do so as a volunteer, or as I would rather call them: *an unpaid professional.* Whether paid and insured or unpaid and uninsured, the best practices are still to document everyone's comings and goings. Accurate and timely record keeping are attributes of a world-class Response Leader.

Once the requested resources have arrived, signed in, and officially become part of the incident, they need organizing.

Event Level

At the event level resources can be organized geographically or functionally.

Geographic Example:

Organize all of the resources that are supporting the event at the North end of the stadium under the North Branch Director. Janitors, paramedics, and referees all serve under the North Branch Director.

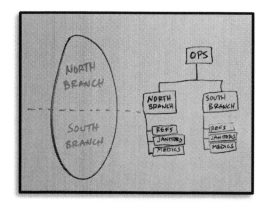

Note: In practice, the designations of "Refs, Janitors, and Medics" need different radio call signs to distinguish their assigned branch.

Functional Example:

All of the medics report to the Medical Branch Director. All of the Janitors report to the Janitorial Branch Director.

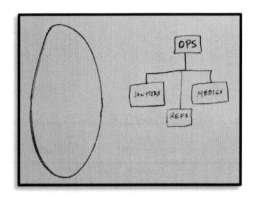

Neither solution is always right nor always wrong.

Emergency Support Functions or ESF's are a more stylized and universal method to label these support functions. There are 15 of them, primarily:

ESF #1 – Transportation
ESF #2 – Communications
ESF #3 – Public Works and Engineering
ESF #4 – Firefighting
ESF #5 – Emergency Management
ESF #6 – Mass Care, Emergency Assistance, Housing, and Human Services
ESF #7 – Logistics Management and Resource Support
ESF #8 – Public Health and Medical Services
ESF #9 – Search and Rescue
ESF #10 – Oil and Hazardous Materials Response
ESF #11 – Agriculture and Natural Resources
ESF #12 – Energy
ESF #13 – Public Safety and Security
ESF #14 – Long-Term Community Recovery

ESF #15 – External Affairs

Some jurisdictions choose to create additional ESF's for their special projects and such, but the fifteen above are by far the most common. Which one do you most align with in your role?

One of the advantages of using ESF's or something equivalent is that it can simplify the identification and organization of large groups of resources.

Example:

Under the Operations Section Chief, the Response Leader organized all security and law enforcement related resources under an ESF 13 Public Safety and Security Branch.

Organizational Level

At the organizational level, the Resource Unit Leader in the Planning Section manages the status of resources. They maintain the most current Sign-In and dispatch logs that show who is officially part of the event.

The Resource Unit Leader also passes these records to the person or people who are managing the Finance and Administrative Function to account for each resource's time (Time Unit), their cost (Cost Unit) and any other injury, reimbursement or another accounting measure (Compensation & Claims Unit).

At the end of an event, this is how Response Leaders identify the amount of money spent on the event.

Example:

The tournament staff - 20 people - arrived at 7 am on the first day of the tournament and signed in at the Staging Area.
They all signed out at 5 pm, totaling 10 hours of service.
Two of them earn $10 per hour, and the rest are volunteers.
One widget was broken and had to be replaced, costing $50.

- 20 staff accounted for

- $200 accounted for paid staff
- $0 accounted for volunteer staff
- $50 accounted for equipment replacement

All of the documentation for those resources is compiled, along with other event-related expenses to account for the cost of the event.

Tactical Level

The importance of resource accountability is no greater than it is at the tactical level.

The Response Leaders in the field, doing the work, achieving the objectives. Sometimes their risk is low, like at a bake sale and sometimes their risk is high, like at a tornado response.

In all cases, *Response Leaders are judged by their ability to deliver all resources back home to their families.*

Personnel Accountability Report (PAR)

Because this is not a responder level program, more specific discussion on the specifics of small unit tactics and field operations are available as part of some of my other programs available at TEAM-Solutions.US.

So while several strategies exist for managing resources in the field, the one I will focus on is called a PAR or Personnel Accountability Report.

These PARs provide quick snapshots of the status of a team. PARs are useful when a supervisor, especially one that does not have regular audio or visual contact with their resources, needs to verify that their team is okay, to get a status on progress and to learn about any unmet needs.

Example:

"Team 1, this is Base - what is your PAR?"

"This is Team 1; we have a PAR with eight members. We are all in good standing with no unmet needs. We are 75% complete with our task and expect to be back in the base in 1 hour."

PARs can be used to communicate any number of brief and relevant topics, but the PAR check's primary focus is on accountability and member safety.

PAR checks are typically done every 30 minutes to an hour so they can be easily scheduled and are not overly burdensome to the field team.

Management of Event Places

"Workers will always expand to fill the space available to them."
~ Deal's Derivative

The event management organization is scalable, and so are the places (facilities) that support them.

After Hurricane Ike in 2008, for example, there were several large but adjacent parking lots in Galveston, Texas occupied with trailers, tents, vehicles, and hundreds and hundreds of people there to support the response.

Everything and everyone there has a purpose, and at the peak of the response, the size of this city-within-a-city was at its peak also.

On the other hand, managing a regional training event for 100 people off of the tailgate of a pickup truck is also 'right-sized.'

Remember, everything that scales up in size can also scale down in size depending on the event requirements.

Facility and Land Use Agreements

If an incident response requires the use of a parking lot, mentioned above, or a building, a formal agreement needs to be in place between the property or landowner and the responders that wish to use it.

Two common agreements for these purposes are:

1. Facility Use Agreement
2. Land Use Agreement

They accomplish the same thing so I'll summarize them both.

When the management of an incident expands beyond the tailgate of the pickup truck, and responders need a place to park, to camp, to stage and to store stuff, nearby and vacant facilities can provide ideal accommodations.

For Hurricane Katrina, we camped at a large sports complex just outside of town. Someone within our command structure made contact with someone who controlled that site and asked if we could use it. These discussions cover topics such as:

- Who will lock and unlock the gate?
- Who will empty the trash?
- Who will service the bathrooms?
- Who will turn the lights on and off?
- Who will repair the carpet if someone spills coffee on it?
- Who will replace the light pole if we back a truck into it?
- How much will it cost, if at all, for the use of the building?
- How long will the facility be occupied?

This verbal agreement is put into writing and becomes the basis of the Facility or Land Use Agreement.

These agreements are usually executed between the property representative and the Procurement Unit Leader in the Finance Section.

Executing a Facility or Land Use Agreement greatly reduces misunderstandings and friction by memorializing verbal agreements into a binding, written one.

Examples of Event Places

Some standard event-related facilities are below. Each name is from the ICS nomenclature:

Staging Area: This is where resources go to await their assignment. If they're in the Staging Area, they should already be assembled and equipped to leave from there to travel to their work assignment. A Staging Area may be as unremarkable as a parking space where Sam and his crew are waiting to put out barricades along the parade route. Or as involved as the one we used during our response to Hurricane Ike. Staging Areas and managed by the Operations Section.

Incident Check-in: This is very similar to a Staging Area. When lots of resources are arriving at the same time, it's advisable to separate where they check-in and where they stage. This procedure allows whoever is checking them in to communicate to the Staging Manager where inside the Staging Area they should go to optimize their departure when receiving their assignment.

Perimeter: This refers to the imaginary line that separates where the work is taking place and where the general public is. In the parade example, a perimeter may be designated by traffic cones. In a tournament, it may be the cyclone fencing that already surrounds the fields. For a cyber-attack, a perimeter may be the door of conference room #3 where the cyber sleuths have gathered to investigate the breach. The sooner you can post these perimeters for all to see, the sooner they can be obeyed!

Camp: Often referred to as a Base Camp, but not the same as an Incident Base. A geographical site within the general incident area (separate from the Incident Base) that is equipped and staffed to provide sleeping, food, water, and sanitary services to incident personnel.

- Resources in a Base Camp belong to the incident but are not available until they arrive at the Staging Area.

Medical Aid / Responder Rehab: These refer to facilities where responders, not the general public, go to receive medical care, rehabilitate with shade, food, water, etc. In large events, there may be more than one. In small events, this function may co-locate at the Staging Area or even Base Camp. These are typically for active resources that need attention, not those who are off-duty.

Incident Command Post (ICP): This is where the event is managed and is near the event itself (for greater situational awareness!)

- Access should be limited to command and general staff but can occasionally host other functional roles depending on the size of the facility.
- Command Posts may be as large as a gym or auditorium or small as the bed of a pick-up truck.

- The importance of a command post is in its ability to manage the event, regardless of how pretty it is.

Emergency Operations Center (EOC): This facility exists solely to support and coordinate the needs of the Incident Command Post (ICP). If the ICP needs people or things that are not readily available to them inside their perimeter, they contact the EOC.

- Few facilities mean more to the success of an event than ICPs and, when needed, EOCs. However, they're often confused or unknowingly used in a manner that decreases efficiency.

Therefore, let's address them in greater detail.

ICP v. EOC

ICPs and EOCs are different. Different in where they are and different in what they do.

Below are some important distinctions based on a typical setup.

Incident Command Post (ICP):

- An ICP is incident specific, exists only as long as the incident, and is where incident commanders make decisions about how to manage the incident.
- An ICP is near the source of the incident, so it is close to the problem it is there to solve.
- An ICP is sometimes in a mobile command center converted from a motor home, or it may be the tailgate of someone's pickup truck.
- Unified commanders and those responsible for managing the incident may be in the ICP; any others are in the way.
- An ICP's management decisions are limited to what occurs inside the incident perimeter.

Emergency Operations Center (EOC):

- An EOC is a support and coordination facility for emergencies that exceed the capability of the ICP. Many large cities have an EOC, and most counties have an EOC.
- An EOC may be unstaffed unless there's an emergency. Some jurisdictions designate people to staff an EOC for an instance when they're needed, and some employ a limited but full-time staff that monitors their jurisdiction for emergent events.
- An EOC is usually inside a brick-and-mortar building like a public safety building or another government complex with comfortable chairs, climate control, and flush toilets.
- Government officials like mayors, department heads that contribute support, and outside agencies brought in for assistance may have a chair in or near the EOC.
- An EOC's management decisions are limited to what occurs in their jurisdiction but outside of the incident perimeter.

	ICP	EOC
Manages the Incident & ICP	✔	-
Supports and *Coordinates* the Incident & ICP's unmet needs	-	✔
Located NEAR the Incident	✔	-
Located AWAY from the Incident	-	✔
Manages activities OUTSIDE the Incident Perimeter	-	✔
Manages activities INSIDE the Incident Perimeter	✔	-

© TEAM-Solutions.US

Example:

306

The Acme Warehouse in Smithville is on fire. The Smithville Fire Department responds. Initially, they size up the problem, define an incident perimeter and begin their fire attack.

Chief Garza is the on-scene Incident Commander. She designates the location of the Incident Command Post to be in the parking lot across the street from the fire out of the back of her command vehicle, a large SUV.

The Smith County EOC may be monitoring the radio traffic of this incident but does not activate any additional resources.

The warehouse fire grows larger unexpectedly due to some unreported flammable chemicals inside.

This escalation creates some unmet needs:

The complexity of this chemical fire prompts Chief Garza to request the Hazardous Materials firefighters from neighboring Jonesburg.
She also needs the residents of the downwind apartment complex to be evacuated and sheltering arranged.
She also requests arson investigators from the state police after she received a report about one of her firefighter's suspicious findings.

Chief Garza communicates these unmet needs to the EOC for their support and coordination.

The EOC captures Chief Garza's incident objectives and activates the necessary resources to support and coordinate the ICP's requests.

If there's another fire in Smithville, a shelter or family assistance center is set up, or a Joint Information Center (JIC) for arriving media opens, the EOC is responsible for coordinating and supporting those activities.

The worsening Acme Warehouse fire needs Chief Garza's attention. By requesting support and coordination from the EOC, she's able to focus on that incident and still have the related needs met.

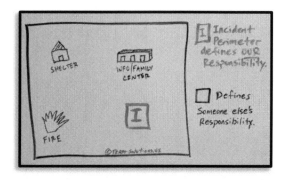

While not ideal, jurisdictions with limited resources, facilities, and money often blend how they designate, staff and manage their EOCs and their ICPs.

Even when the jurisdiction can operate a separate EOC and ICP, the line between them is still often blurred and therefore complicated.

The reasons are predictable too. It's common practice and even expected that the most experienced field commanders are eventually 'promoted' to a position at the EOC.

Therefore, it's within reason that Chief Garza from Smithville from our previous case-study is asked to serve at the EOC during a large incident occurring in neighboring Jonesburg.

However, Chief Garza's breadth of experience is in her incident command skills, not in supporting and coordinating other resources from a mile away while in air-conditioned comfort.

Similarly, the assigned Jonesburg incident commander may be inexperienced serving in that role. As a result, they may not vocalize when someone in the EOC oversteps their bounds.

This disparity forms the basis for a common misstep in the EOC / ICP interface: someone from the EOC abandoning their coordinate and support role to delve into trying to command and control the incident.

Some may argue that we should 'put our best foot forward' when lives are at stake.

However, besides the arrogance of feeling that our way is always the best way, two major problems are created if Chief Garza tries to direct the Jonesburg incident from the EOC:

If Chief Garza is directing the incident, then she is not performing the critical incident needs that the EOC should be supporting and coordinating.

The EOC lacks the same 'ground truth' as the ICP so making command decisions without proper situational awareness is problematic at best and negligent at worst.

Executive Policy Group

An Executive Policy Group guides the Incident Commander and the EOC in policy matters, obviously.

Universities and other large public institutions like transit authorities have an Executive Policy Group or EPG.

In the example of civil unrest on campus, the EPG would guide those managing the emergency on matters concerning human relations, evacuations, legal issues like curfews, school closures, public media statements, etc.

While the EPG may be in the same building as the EOC, they are usually most useful to the incident when they convene separately from the EOC. In that case, the EOC's Liaison officer or EOC Manager would be responsible for communicating with them and keeping them informed.

Here's a visual of all of the relationships together.

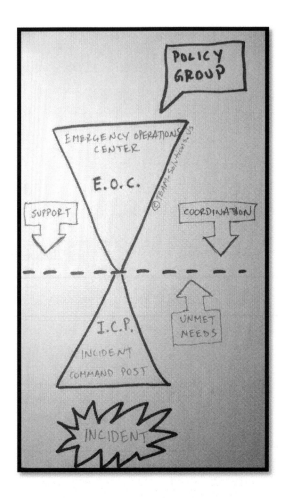

Despite the acronyms and nuances, what a Response Leader ultimately calls a facility is not nearly as important as everyone understanding what role the facility performs.

Management of People

> "Unless someone like you
> cares a whole awful lot,
> nothing is going
> to get better. It's not."
> ~ Ted Geisel (Dr. Seuss)

After identifying and requesting resources, there should be a system to support them once they arrive.

Even if they are expected to be self-supporting when they arrive, the Response Leaders know the value of people that come to help (also known as 'force multipliers'). Therefore, they will make it as comfortable for them as possible.

If Aunt Jean invited you to her house for the weekend and she didn't have any food or a place to sleep for you would you enjoy the experience and want to come back?

Me neither!

A typical pinch-point in a large event is the Staging Area, as described in a separate lesson.

In many cases, the Staging Area is also a suitable location to provide a briefing on the event and share other important information while everyone is together.

Support Considerations for People, Places, and Things

The top considerations for properly supporting the resources that are supporting you:

1. Supporting adequate Work / Rest Cycles.
2. Identifying adequate food, water, and hygiene facilities.
3. Designating a Base Camp for them to spend their off-duty or overnight hours.
4. Designating a Staging Area or check-in location for them to arrive and prepare for their work assignment.
5. Clear and accurate action plans that identify at a minimum:
    a. The event objectives.
    b. Relevant contacts and hierarchy.
    c. A re-supply plan.
    d. A medical plan in case of injury.
    e. A communication plan on how they will communicate.
6. Frequent communication on the event status, including when you expect it to end!

Communications

"The problem with communication is the illusion that is has occurred." ~ George Bernard Shaw

---

"How did the event go?"
"Great."

"Were there any problems?"
"Well, the left hand seldom knew what the right hand was doing."

- When people feel isolated by not having access to relevant information, they start to disengage because they don't feel respected by those with the pertinent information.
- A disengaged team member is not productive.
- And when people are not productive, objectives don't get met.

So, really now, how did the event go? *"Okay, it was pretty rotten. I doubt most people will want to participate again."*

Perhaps that's too harsh. However, since there are no perfect events, if we were to list the factors that made it imperfect, poor communication would lead the list.

Here are some strategies to improve Response Leader communication.

Active Listening

When a big building collapses, disaster responders race to the scene to search the rubble pile for survivors. People who are trapped and are able to call out to searchers will be easier to find because they're heard and can direct help to their location.

However other trapped people may be injured or deeply entombed and not easily heard. To find them, we will deploy a technique called active listening.

Active listening detects the sounds and signals that most people miss.

- Active listening is simply a strategy where we reduce or eliminate all other noise and focus on one part of the rubble pile at a time.
- We can increase our chance of detecting and locating what we're looking for simply by listening for any audio anomaly.

Some of the challenges to be successful at active listening is audio contamination from other rescue operations (jackhammers, cranes, barking search dogs, etc.) and of course, there has to be an actual sound to hear.

We can refine what we hear and where we hear it by using acoustic (airborne sounds) and seismic (structure-borne sounds) detection equipment.

And this exact active listening strategy can also help Response Leaders find what they're looking for too.

Example:

When investigating discord among team members, instead of demanding that the team share what's going on, a Response Leader can use their active listening skills to detect the origin of the friction.

Instead of interjecting comments during a staff meeting, a Response Leader can use their active listening skills to evaluate the strengths and weaknesses of the plan and the people implementing the plan.

Active listening detects the sounds and signals that most people miss.

Crisis Communications

Crisis Communications has gathered a lot of interest in the last several years.

There is a 'right-to-know' mentality in the general public that demands information on any issue or crisis they choose.

- Vastly misunderstood is that the "Right-to-Know" doctrine, or Emergency Planning and Community Right-to-Know Act (EPCRA), applies only to the public's right to be notified if the government or industry is building a nuclear power plant or storing hazardous materials in their neighborhood.
- The doctrine's rights do not extend to whatever the public feels entitled to know.

Nonetheless, if an accurate account from the source is not available, then inaccurate accounts from the peanut gallery on social media, etc. will fill in the blanks.

Some considerations that a Response Leader should address when communicating with the public and their internal audience:

1. **Start with empathy** - humanity in the face of crisis builds trust and credibility.
2. **Deliver the facts** - dispel myths and rumors by providing a factual account of the event. If you don't know, say you don't know then get back to them.
3. **Lead from the front** - take responsibility with courage and confidence.
4. **Provide direction** - let the public know where to go to get more information, support, etc.
5. **Promote solidarity** - when a crisis impacts the community, the community can also work together to lessen the impact.

Some crisis communication advice suggests that one of the elements is a profuse apology and a public-centered plea for forgiveness regardless of their role in the crisis.

While I respect many of these crisis communication consultants, I don't agree with that advice, unless there is truly something to apologize for of course.

Sometimes, however, bad things happen to good people. Being empathetic is important because tomorrow it could be us. Being apologetic is not the same thing as being empathetic.

A Response Leader communicating during a crisis needs to remember that they did not create the disaster so apologizing for it comes across as powerless. And the public wants their Response Leaders to be in control, not powerless.

<u>Example:</u>

*"Let me start by saying that our thoughts and prayers are with the Woodhaven neighborhood tonight during this time of loss and tragedy (**EMPATHY**). Here's what we know: at 9 am today a cement truck left the roadway at the intersection of 1st and Main. It crashed into the side of the city's recreation center; four occupants inside of the recreation center lost their lives. We are withholding their names until after we notify the victim's families. There were six people injured, including the driver of the cement truck, who were transported to local hospitals. (**FACTS**) The police department's accident investigation team is thoroughly investigating this accident, and early reports are that the cement truck was operating above the speed limit and that driver impairment may be a factor. We will pursue all legal remedies against the driver and the cement company as appropriate. We will also be evaluating the traffic pattern, speed zones and safety barriers in that area to see if any changes are needed to reduce the chance of anything like this from happening again. (**LEADERSHIP**) The recreation center will remain closed until the investigation is complete and repairs are made likely for at least four weeks. Contact us at this number or at this website to learn where and when the scheduled recreation classes will resume. (**DIRECTION**) Before I open the floor for questions, I'd like to commend the Woodhaven community for supporting our response efforts and for providing support to the families directly impacted by today's tragic event." (**SOLIDARITY**)*

Functional Communications

While conducting the business of the event, from the command and general staff level down to the lowest tactical assignment, the ability to communicate effectively is a pillar of all masterful Response Leaders.

View these functional communications as more of a running faucet than as gas and brake pedals.

Facilitating the constant flow of information up and down the organization structure is one of the most effective ingredients for other Response Leaders to understand and support the mission.

Here are some highlights of successful functional communications:

Common Language

There's a book out there called the F.A.A.T. Book.

It's 78 pages of approximately 6500 glorious and mind-numbing acronyms, abbreviations, and terms used by the United States Federal Emergency Management Agency (FEMA). I kid you not.

The full title is:

"FEMA Acronyms Abbreviations and Terms"

- You likely noticed the oozing irony.
- Yes, it is a book about acronyms, abbreviations, and terms, whose title is an acronym (F.A.A.T. Book) that contains an acronym (F.E.M.A.).

I cannot make this stuff up.

If you ever find yourself in a position where you have to carry around the F.A.A.T. Book to communicate, something has gone very, very wrong.

Common language refers to speaking plainly, without codes, jargon or other impediments to comprehension.

When a crime of national significance occurs, who do you prefer to appear: the Federal Bureau of Investigation (FBI) ... or a Food Borne Illness (FBI)?

Kidding aside, this is harder than we think. We're all a sum of our experiences so with exposure to years of industry jargon; we likely use it without really noticing it. This manner of speaking is particularly the case with people that are like us.

Seeing others with a different background turn their head like a puppy who heard a squeak is an indication that we said something foreign.

It's also an indicator to have our event operation come to a screeching halt because someone delivered Plastic Wicker Stools and Tables (PWST) to the ruptured gas line instead of a Public Works Strike Team (PWST).

Another common trap in our pursuit of a common language is the assumption that what is commonly known to us is commonly known to other people too.

Example:

Team 1 calls in on the radio that they "detected the odor of mercaptan." Because one person may know that the smell of mercaptan is an indicator of a natural gas leak and therefore a very hazardous environment that requires evacuation, that doesn't mean that everyone else knows that too.

Imprinting the following question can help guard against this type of communication:

"Who else needs this information?"

When we are always pushing ourselves and others to share, share and share some more with other Response Leaders, we're more apt to discover sooner rather than later when we communicate something confusing or incomplete.

So as we see, a common language is not very common. To correct this, Response Leaders must model the communication they expect from others.

Myth of Interoperability

Interoperability refers to system A being able to communicate with system B.

Seems logical on the surface, except that systems don't communicate, people communicate.

That's why Response Leaders have come to realize that interoperability is a myth.

To illustrate the failure of interoperability, think of the last time you or your loved one went to the doctor. Even though you have been to the same doctor for ten years and even though your insurance has not changed, 20 minutes of each annual visit involves filling out hordes of the same paperwork that you filled out last year. Same information. Same form. All while holding a smartphone in your other hand that can synchronize your email across 17 different devices and can control an orbital satellite reliably and securely within seconds. The technology has been around for a long, long time to be able to record, store, update, view, and transfer medical records safely. Nonetheless, the embarrassing lack of working relationships in the medical records business keeps the process in the dark ages.

Just because my radio can talk to Bill's radio, doesn't mean I want to key the mic to speak to Bill. Or vice versa.

Even if the technology worked well together (rarely does it), relationships are what defines true interoperability, not technology.

Response leaders know to build the relationships first and the technology second. When (not if) the latter fails, the former will still light the way to a solution.

Technology

As with the topic of interoperability, the presence or absence of technology has its challenges.

Before the widespread use of technology, communication was slow, prone to error and often unverified.

Now with technology present and available in virtually every part of our lives, communication is fast, prone to error and often unverified.

The speed has changed, but our ability to understand has not changed with it.

Anything I wrote about the highest form of communication technology would likely be outdated by the time I pressed 'save,' so instead, I'm going the opposite direction.

What is the lowest form of communication technology? If you said "pen and paper" or even "face-to-face" communication, congratulations. If the world were to go mad and all technology were to die, the Response Leaders who can form a sentence on paper and speak to someone while looking in their eyes will likely inherit the earth.

Redundancy

Technology is in every part of our lives for some excellent and helpful reasons. As Response Leaders, we should embrace how some of it can even make our events and our communication go more smoothly.

However, relying on only one form of technology for anything is perilous. Remember this poem:

3 is 2
2 is 1
1 is none

If you only have one form of communications technology, when it fails so too does your ability to communicate.

And since communication is a leading cause of operational friction, having redundant interfaces is required.

Different types of recommended communication:

- Radio
- Landline Phone
- Mobile Text
- Satellite phone
- Email
- Mobile apps
- Written notes/forms
- Posted notices
- Face-to-face
- Smoke signals
- Etc.?

Meetings vs. Briefings

A subtle but important distinction exists between meeting and briefings.

- **Meetings are 2-way communication**. During a meeting, respectful and relevant contributions are usually acceptable. Meetings are prime time to cuss and discuss details, plans, and strategies.
- **Briefings are 1-way communication**. When a Response Leader briefs, the audience should not interrupt and instead take notes of the briefing to capture important details. Questions, if allowed, can occur at the end of the briefing. As a notable mentor of mine says: "Be brief and be gone."

Example:

Meeting: After the Trigger of an event response, initial Response Leaders will facilitate a meeting to discuss what objectives need documenting. Contributions are invited and expected.

Briefing: Onboard an airline flight, the flight crew will present a flight safety briefing where they pass along relevant information along. Interruptions are not appropriate.

Briefings are an essential tool in the Response Leader's tool bag. By packaging valuable information into a streamlined briefing, The Response Leadership Sequence™ can continue at a steady clip.

Examples of items covered in a briefing:

- Current Event Status
- Review of the Objectives
- Safety Concerns and Response Procedures
- Description of Tasks
- Location of Event Facilities and Functional Areas
- Communication System
- Expectations
- Description of How to Request More People and Things
- Event Schedule
- Answer Questions and Address Concerns

To gain a deeper and more practical understanding of how to perform a briefing and its mirror opposite debriefing, enroll in the online, advanced communications program called appropriately "Briefing and Debriefing for Better Communication" at TEAM-Solutions.US.

By balancing the use of briefings and meetings, Response Leaders can maximize people's time and opportunity to understand the material.

Formal vs. Informal Communications

The best way to communicate should always first be measured by whether the recipient understood the information. If not, adding or subtracting any formality likely won't fix that.

There are two principal communication categories a Response Leader uses:

1. **Formal** - these are structured and facilitated meetings or briefings where there may be an agenda, a speaker at a podium, a recording made, etc. Formal communication creates a record and may also consist of emails, printed memos or display boards. There are typically rules and expectations when giving or receiving formal communication.

2. **Informal** - these are water-cooler discussions and other non-official communication. Some may be rumor-mongering: "Hey, did you hear that Russ is getting fired for stealing?" However, informal communication is also a critical aspect of relationship building and engagement: "Hey, what do you think about the best way to move this paper from one side of the desk to another?"

Flagging every conversation as being either formal or informal is not the goal here; understanding that these categories of communication have different results is.

Balance (or Imbalance) of Information Sharing

In a perfect world, information flows freely up and down the organization, gathering speed and accuracy as it goes.

In the real world though, obstacles exist that impede this flow. Some are big, and some are small.

One of the more significant impediments is the thorny relationship between the dominance of the Response Leader and the willingness for people to share information.

When the balance has gained too much mass on one side, the other side tends to lose mass.

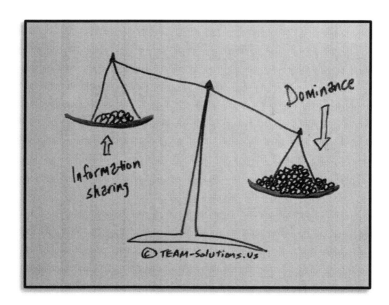

Common indicators of too much dominance on the Response Leadership side:

- Lower level workers are discouraged from communicating with high-level workers.

- Higher-level workers have separate office space, parking, eating areas, etc.
- Too many one-way briefings, not enough meetings.
- Too much arrogance, not enough humility.

Note too that this isn't about Unity of Command or Chain of Command. Those constructs exist for excellent reasons.

Balancing the flow of information recognizes that some formal and nearly all informal communications should be unrestricted between all levels of the organization.

Information Management

"The new source of power is not money in the hands of a few, but information in the hands of many. " ~ John Naisbitt

---

When lots of important work takes place, it often results in lots of important information.

This information may come in the form of:

- Handwritten reports
- Computer data including databases, emails, etc.
- Texts and other mobile data
- Meeting minutes
- Planning worksheets
- Sign in forms
- ICS documents galore
- Etc.

With an ocean of data in front of them, the Response Leader must first recognize what data is information and what data is intelligence.

Understanding the difference is helpful in decision-making and strategy.

Information vs. Intelligence

Information is:

1. data that is usually unconfirmed
2. does little to drive our objectives and The Response Leadership Sequence™ forward
3. is usually tactical in nature (i.e., directions, tools, checklists, etc.)

Intelligence is:

1. verified data
2. does drive our objectives and The Response Leadership Sequence™ forward
3. can fuel better strategic decisions (i.e., how to develop a process, implement a plan, maximize a system, etc.)

Example:

"Johnny saw on Facebook that some anarchists intend to hack companies in our industry this weekend."

"The FBI (Federal Bureau of Investigation) issued this bulletin this morning that a known hacker group listed the names of companies that they will be attacking this weekend. We are on that list."

The first example, information obviously, is still relevant. It just needs verification before any significant action occurs.

Before distributing intelligence, it should carry the following characteristics:

1. **It has a timestamp**
2. **It has an author or source listed for follow-up**
3. **It clearly indicates whether it is confirmed or not confirmed**

Similarly, a percentage of accuracy, such as, *"I am 70% confident"* gives the recipient a realistic measurement before making a decision based on that intelligence.

The role of a Situation Unit, as discussed earlier, is invaluable in gathering and filtering information into usable intelligence.

Once the data is deemed important enough to document as part of the event, the next question is to determine what is part of the JOB and what is merely a JOB AID.

Jobs vs. Job Aids

JOB: In Search and Rescue, an annotated and hand-drawn map with what the searcher did and didn't do is not only valuable, but it can drastically enhance our efforts to find lost Little Timmy. A map, in this case, IS an essential element of the job.

JOB AID: A reference manual to take home at the end of a training class. That's a job aid because you can most likely perform the learned behavior without relying on the manual.

Jobs and job aids are both important, and both have their place.

In fact, a job aid that is extremely helpful and that I regularly use for all kinds of projects:

Checklists!

For routine tasks, checklists can be the ultimate job aid.

When time is limited, make sure you know the difference between jobs and job aids so that you always focus on the JOB first.

There are as many variables to manage information as there are types of information, so it's unrealistic to address all of them here.

Utilization of the ICS forms previously mentioned provide a sensible and common Information Management strategies.

One of the simplest and most accepted is to use a sign-in form any time resources are gathered that shows:

- WHAT the event name is
- WHO signed in
- WHAT organization they are with
- WHEN they signed in (date and time)
- WHEN they signed out

Communication Summary

High-functioning Response Leaders are always poised to ask themselves two (2) questions relating to communications and information management:

When they receive any new information, they ask themselves: ***"who else needs to know this?"***

- They use display boards, ICS forms, technology, sky-writers and public-address announcements to do their part to share relevant information.

When they need new information, they ask themselves: ***"where do I go to get it?"***

- Since they recruited the best of the best, they know that someone else is always smarter than they are on any given topic. So, the Response Leader seeks out the subject matter expert to assist with any topic where the Response Leader needs information and clarity.

These high-functioning Response Leaders understand that communication works best when built on solid relationships. They also understand that managing information works best when it utilizes standardized and well-understood processes.

Response Resolution

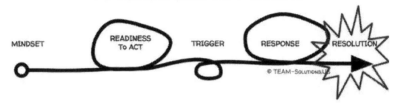

How and When does it all End?

There was a popular comedy show on TV when I was a kid called Gilligan's Island. It featured an eclectic cast of 7 people that boarded a small boat for a 3-hour tour. A mere 3-hour tour.

Shortly after leaving port, a storm washed them out to sea, and they all became stranded on a deserted island together for years and years - in TV time anyway.

Why did I share that?

I shared that because one of the hidden dangers of leading a response is having it morph into a Gilligan's Island response. One that promised to be a manageable 3-hour tour but instead became a year lost at sea on a deserted island eating bugs.

Starting with and continually refining your objectives is the best way to avoid this.

Example:

- Say your objective was to "clean up the spilled coffee, refill the coffee pot, throw away the dirty paper towels before going back to your desk."
- When you complete those SMART-ish objectives, your response is over.

However, if there are still objectives that need accomplishing, new and fresh Response Leaders may be necessary.

Transfer of Command

"Leaders don't inflict pain; they share pain." ~ *Max De Pree*

When an event is long in duration, a more experienced leader arrives on the scene, or our usefulness has decreased due to fatigue, personal emergency, etc. then transferring our command to another leader is appropriate.

Done in person and augmented in writing, the outgoing commander will brief the incoming commander on notable accomplishments, remaining gaps, and their informed recommendations.

See also my Communications program on effective Briefing and Debriefing at TEAM-Solutions.US.

This process of transferring command takes place until we have accomplished all of the objectives.

For instance, during the response to address the aftermath of Hurricane Katrina, our commanders transferred command every ten days to new, fresh teams. This transfer of command went on until we accomplished all of the search and rescue objectives.

Besides completing our objectives, there may be other reasons why we complete our response and go home, also known as being 'demobilized':

- A more qualified person or team arrives, like an Incident Management Team.
- Your commitment to maintaining an adequate work/rest cycle dictates that you demobilize.
- Someone higher up the food chain dictates that a transfer of leadership takes place.

Hot Wash

"Our bravest and best lessons are not learned through success, but through misadventure." ~ Amos Bronson Alcott

---

But what if yours was the 2nd coffee spill of the day and it spilled because all of the coffee cups are old and cracked and prone to leak or spill?

If left unchecked, that same condition (cracked cups) will inevitably cause more spills tomorrow.

That matters to Response Leaders and risk managers who are always looking for an opportunity to improve.

Or maybe the cup spilled because the workspaces are too close together and your office-mate bangs his chair against your desk every time he gets up?

The initial process to identify improvements is referred to as a "Hot Wash" which originates from the decontamination process where dirty stuff is washed off with hot water before it sticks.

Hot Washes can occur around the bed of a pickup truck, after a client meeting in the car to the airport or at the bar after a conference.

The value is in the authentic, face-to-face sharing of burning issues before they fester and not in the location where the Hot Wash is conducted.

Response leaders don't seek blame they seek improvement. Therefore, the Hot Wash should be brief and focused on what critical issues need hearing immediately.

An example of the Hot Wash process:

1. At the event's onset, communicate that a Hot Wash will likely occur at the end of the response and that attendance is required.

2. Select a private location that accommodates your group of responders.
   a. Make sure the location is away from the ears and eyes of people that were not part of the same response.
3. The facilitator, usually the primary Response Leader, reminds the group that the objective of the Hot Wash is to identify improvements based on the group's experience immediately after the response.
4. If there is tension in the group, emphasize that the Hot Wash should not provoke criticism or seek to determine success or failure. The focus should stay on evaluating the performance, not the people.
5. Ask that contributions are honest, accurate, and reflect their first-hand experience.
6. Select a scribe that will take notes during the discussion for later recall.
7. Some sample questions for the facilitator to ask during a Hot Wash:
   a. *What are some strengths discovered during the response?*
   b. *What are some areas of improvement discovered during the response?*
   c. *What unmet needs were discovered but not planned for?*
   d. *Within your area of responsibility, what immediate corrective actions are recommended?*
8. Remind the participants that the objective is to learn about potential improvements and that their candor is appreciated.
9. Each participant should be given the opportunity to contribute. Afterward, close the meeting and allow them to transition home or wherever they go next.

In the days, weeks or months after a Hot Wash occurs, the next step is a more formal process to capture the factors that enabled the response to go well or not-so-well. The notes from the Hot Wash will come in handy!

This process, addressed shortly, is an After-Action Report (AAR) and an Improvement Plan (IP), which happens after everyone is demobilized and has a chance to reflect back on the response.

Demobilization

"I do not take leave of you, for my spirit will accompany you wherever you may be." ~ *King Ludwig II of Bavaria*

Demobilization is the opposite of being mobilized and essentially means being sent home after serving during a response.

Tasks involved in demobilizing include:

- Turning in all issued equipment
- Reporting any injury or loss
- Filing all activity reports (i.e., ICS 214 Activity Log)
- Submitting reimbursement forms and receipts
- Medical out-processing
- Travel Risk Assessment
- Other Duties as Assigned!
- Etc.

Everyone at some point needs demobilizing, or 'demob-ing.'

For long, arduous or traumatic responses, it's incumbent on everyone - not just the supervisors and safety personnel - to ensure that nobody goes home that poses a risk to themselves or others.

There is no greater tragedy than a responder who just finished working to save lives dying either intentionally by their hand (suicide) or unintentionally (sleep deprived) because we let them leave without addressing their physical and mental health.

Ideally, the planning for demobilization should occur when those resources mobilize. That allows the Response Leaders to plan when and how to let their valuable resources start to transition home safely.

At a minimum, they should be required to sign out just as they signed in. This signing action will create a bookend for the time all participants served the incident and will make any reimbursement more accurate and timely.

On my task force, when responders sign-in upon arrival at the beginning of the response, they turn their car keys in at the same time. When they all demobilize or "demob," only then can they get their keys back from the Safety Officer.

Regardless of the tactic used, nobody should ever be allowed to demob unless he or she can do so safely.

After-Action Report and Improvement Plan

"It takes humility to seek feedback. It takes wisdom to understand it, analyze it, and appropriately act on it." ~ *Stephen R. Covey*

The After-Action Report and Improvement Plan (AAR/IP) are the functions that get put into written form and that memorialize what the Response Leader(s) learned during the event. They also include what concrete steps should be taken to improve.

Homeland Security Exercise and Evaluation Program (HSEEP) is the federal government program that details the AAR/IP process.

- Typically, a third party facilitates the creation of this document or at least someone that was not directly involved in the leadership of the event.
- It should happen as soon as possible after the event and should be honest, accurate and forward-looking.
- Before the next event, carefully review the AAR from the previous event to identify future actions and improvement plans.

If you are not required to conduct a formal HSEEP After-Action Report, the process is still absolutely valuable.

Unfortunately, a common mistake of many, many organizations is to pat themselves on the back after a response, pack away their equipment, send their people home and then move on with their lives.

Not only is ignoring the AAR process irresponsible, but it also guarantees that the deficiencies present in the last response will show themselves in the next response.

Hot Washes, After-Action Reports, and Improvement Plans are crucial tools to improve performance.

Take the time to conduct some version of a Hot Wash, an After-Action Report, and an Improvement Plan. They're the best gifts we can give our future Response Leaders.

Recovery

"Most of our problems can be solved. Some of them will take brains, and some of them will take patience, but all of them will have to be wrestled with like an alligator in the swamp." ~ Harold Washington

---

The focus of Response Leadership is quite obviously on the response and the leadership.

However, for Response Leaders to be successful time after time, there must be some resolution to their previous event(s).

That event, that community, those stakeholders must have all recovered for the Response Leader to be able to put a nice bow on the event.

- Recovering from the proverbial spilled cup of coffee is relatively easy to do.
- Recovering from a Category 4 Hurricane is quite a bit more difficult. Just ask the good people of New Orleans.

So, while recovery measures are outside the scope of this program, it does bear mentioning.

Recovery leaders can and do use the same processes to develop objectives and the same resource leadership techniques to recover from an event.

And when the people, places and things from an event have finally returned to their previous (or better) condition, The Response Leadership Sequence™ ends.

And everybody returns to his or her state of Readiness to Act.

Checklist – The Response Leadership Sequence™

- [ ] Commit to Response Leadership Mindset
- [ ] Build and Maintain a Readiness to Act
  - o D.U.F.F.E.L. B.A.G.
  - o Decision-making models
  - o Wheel of Engagement
  - o Contingency Plans
- [ ] Trigger
- [ ] Respond (Incident Check-In List – ICS 211 and ICS 214 – Activity Log)
- [ ] Notify and activate initial resources
- [ ] Ask and answer (Incident Briefing - ICS 201):
  - o What happened?
  - o Why are we here?
  - o Pillars of Command
- [ ] Start solving the problem
- [ ] Unify other stakeholders
- [ ] Create SMART objectives (Objectives Meeting - ICS 202) based on
  - o life safety
  - o incident stabilization
  - o property preservation
- [ ] Collaborate with other Response Leaders assigned (Command and General Staff Meeting – ICS 202)
- [ ] Define the organization (ICS 203 and 207)
- [ ] Enable and Promote Ongoing Situational Awareness
- [ ] Plan for future people, places, and things, assess their risk. (Tactics Meeting - ICS 202, 215, 215A, 204 and ICS 213 Resource Request)
  - o Define task assignments and resources needed to complete objectives (Operations - ICS 215 and 202)
  - o Conduct risk assessment of the tactics plan (Safety – ICS 215A)
  - o Request additional people and things needed (Logistics – ICS 213RR)
  - o Track resource availability and fill out their assignment sheet (Resource Unit – ICS 204)
- [ ] Huddle with Command and General Staff to confirm the plan (Planning Meeting)
- [ ] Create and Publish Incident Action Plan (IAP) with forms

- Communicate the completed plan to the incoming staff for new operational period (Operations Period Briefing – Completed IAP)
- Work the plan (Operations)
- Revise and Repeat until resolving the problem
- Hot Wash frequently and always before people demobilize
- Identify Gaps and Needed Improvements (AAR/IP)
- Rehab, Restore, and Return to a Readiness to Act

Your Legacy as a Response Leader

"The things you do for yourself are gone when you are gone, but the things you do for others remain as your legacy." ~ Kalu Ndukwe Kalu

---

Higher level Response Leader positions come about from a variety of ways:

1.   We created the position and grew into it.
2.   Someone retired and we inherited his or her position.
3.   Some were promoted (or demoted), and we inherited their position.
4.   Someone left, or the organization grew and needed more leaders.

When someone had a part to play in us advancing into that higher-level leadership role, how was the experience?

Sadly, many people leave a 'legacy' by leaving a wake of distrust and toxicity.

They climb the organizational ladder and then push it down behind them when they reach the top.

If that's our only example of leaving a legacy, we're bound to repeat the pattern.

You will get all you want in life if you help enough other people get what they want. ~ Zig Ziglar

---

The greatest gift a Response Leader can leave after an event is taking a bad condition and returning it in a restored condition.

- How soon is it too soon to start thinking about your legacy?
- Are you going to wait until you near the end of your career and then try to cram in a bunch of noble gestures before receiving your proverbial gold watch?
- Or are you building the ladder now to enable future leaders to climb even higher with your legacy as a guide?

Much of my adult life has been spent serving those around me, particularly in the field of Response Leadership, responding and teaching search and rescue, etc.

Early on, I adopted a motto that has helped me stay focused on the mission:

"Do the most good for the most people as quickly and safely as possible."

That one sentence and mental model has become central to virtually every aspect of my personal and professional life. That, and *"never pass up a bathroom, a meal or a nap,"* but I digress.

The bonus is that I can naturally measure my contributions against that motto, yesterday, today and tomorrow.

So, if my kids and other people I'm able to influence grow-up always striving to serve something bigger than themselves in a meaningful way ... I've been successful, even without a gold watch!

In the spirit of planning, another successful strategy is to look at the legacy that you received from others.

Maybe it's the guy or gal whose job you took over? Did they leave a legacy for you to meet and exceed? How can you leave the job better for the next person?

Maybe it's a parent, teacher, etc.? Did they encourage you to 'improve the breed' (a standard instruction from my father)? How are you building off of their success?

In any case, it's never too soon to envision how you want the world to remember you. And then to lead definitively in that direction.

"What you leave behind is not what is engraved in stone monuments, but what is woven into the lives of others." ~ *Pericles*

Succession Planning and Resiliency

"There is no success without a successor." ~ Peter Drucker

Succession planning isn't just for corporate presidents and monarchs on the throne.

One of the more efficient ways for a Response Leader to leave a lasting legacy it to actively plan for a successor.

Your replacement can take the best parts of what you do and who you are and add them to everything else they know and learn. It's a win-win!

Also, as discussed separately, for any organization to be truly resilient, they must be built around sustainable functions and not "Bob the Handyman."

Succession planning enables organizations to be sustainable and resilient!

Often, potential successors are like ripe fruit and get picked from the top of the blossoming apple tree. That may be necessary of course if the successor needs to take over sooner than later.

However, an often-overlooked strategy is looking at the newly planted tree or seeds that have yet even to sprout.

Whether your potential successor comes from within your current organization or from an entirely different area, the people that you cultivate will be living examples of the kind of person you are.

Mentorship

"Whoever renders service to many puts himself in line for greatness – great wealth, great return, great satisfaction, great reputation, and great joy." ~ Jim Rohn

---

A growing part of my role in Response Leadership these days is spent educating future and current Response Leaders.

It brings me immeasurable joy when I see or hear someone I interacted with succeeding at something we had discussed. It's the payday that keeps paying.

If you have skill and interest in being an educator, consider sharing your knowledge and your talents with others.

Mentoring is engaging so remember that the TEAM Solutions Wheel of Engagement™ is a powerful tool to assist you in serving and mentoring others, too.

I'll add that whether you call it instructing, teaching, educating, coaching, or mentoring, the students deserve your very best. Remember, they will learn something from you regardless so be sure it's your best work.

My passion project the past couple of years has been sharing instructor guidance, techniques and insights via a free newsletter. To join the community, I invite you to join for free on my website, TEAM-Solutions.US.

BONUS MATERIAL

The material in this book is also presented in a comprehensive, interactive and innovative online program.

Click below or navigate to **https://team-solutions.us/response-leadership-training-program-lp/**

The Response Leadership Program™

Participants in the online program receive access to all of the forms, checklists, and other job aids mentioned in this book.

Readers of this book that also leave a review receive a **20% discount** on enrollment by entering **"RLPBook20"** during checkout.

Most of these documents are also available as a separate download.

Connect with me, share your results, and **sign-up for more free leadership content** by visiting TEAM-Solutions.US

Thank you for reading, for your support, and for sharing with your network.

Mike.

Made in the USA
Columbia, SC
24 December 2018